12 Steps To
flow

The New Framework for Business Agility

Haydn Shaughnessey & Fin Goulding

1st Edition June 2018

ISBN Paperback: 978-1-9995906-0-4
ISBN eBook: 978-1-9995906-1-1

Printed in the United States of America and United Kingdom

Cover Design: Anna Jarvis
Interior Design: Fusion Creative Works, www.fusioncw.com

Praise for *Flow*

In *Flow*, Fin Goulding and Haydn Shaughnessy provide a wonderful combination of principles and practices for technology leaders, not only for improving their teams' outcomes, but to help them bring all their other business stakeholders along on the journey, too. Highly recommended.

— **Gene Kim, co-author** ***The Phoenix Project*** **and** ***The DevOps Handbook***

In *Flow*, Haydn Shaughnessy and Fin Goulding provide a clear roadmap for establishing the business agility needed to compete in today's complex environment of digital transformation. Through practical real-world examples and drawing on their considerable depth of corporate experience, the authors provide invaluable concepts and tools to establish a culture of value based on customer centricity.

— **Rob Smart, Former Dean, Walgreens University**

Ever wondered why your Agile journey has not delivered the outcomes you were looking for? Fin and Haydn take you beyond the process, planning and control thinking of the past in this practical toolkit laying out how to execute on digital transformation. Reading *Flow* will make you wish you'd applied the logic, tools and insights earlier. Do however be prepared to re-think some old habits! *Flow* is all about creating the right culture for change through real empowerment, team diversity and interactive visual engagement and constant feedback loops. Easy to read, well-structured and frequently used for reference. Highly recommended for anyone involved in delivering change, especially for those who wonder why innovation does not happen.

— Mark Simons, Global Cloud Programme
Director, Aviva Plc

Flow and Flow Academy offer tremendous value to anyone looking to transform the way their teams and organisations work. Thought provoking guidance that challenges me to rethink everything.

— Jim Dolce, VP Technology Strategy
FujiFilm North America

A lot is written about how Agile and Lean supports faster and more efficient software development, often describing how to do the wrong things faster. *Flow* is about how to introduce Agile and Lean to deliver the "right" things faster. Fin and Haydn show practical ways to get whole organizations (not just development) thinking and solving customers problems, then flawlessly flowing that value to those customers.

— Troy Magennis: Founder/Metrics & Forecasting
Consultant, Focused Objective

The essence of agility is enabling new behaviors and thinking to emerge throughout your organization. Fin and Haydn outline an actionable yet minimal framework to innovate your ways of working and create a culture of experimentation and learning. The lessons, methods and tools shared in this book will provide you with an effective guide to succeed on your own journey towards higher performance, better results and flow.

— **Barry O'Reilly, founder of ExecCamp, author of *Unlearn* and *Lean Enterprise***

I really enjoyed reading the ideas from Fin and Haydn, ideas that have been tried and tested. I love the Executive Wall, and the other walls that radiate information from concept through to customer value realisation. I love the focus on customer feedback via the Customer Feedback Wall. Fin and Haydn observed correctly that the incorrect application of Scrum is commonplace, and I also believe from my experience that flow is the tip of the spear, reducing the number of products, initiatives, backlog items in progress, as long as we talk to external customers to collect feedback the way Fin and Haydn say we must. A must read for executives, and leaders at all levels.

— **John Coleman, Agile Strategist**

In the race for agile transformation somebody has to spell out what the enterprise looks like once many more people are empowered. At last, in Flow we have that document and with it the start of a movement for a new way to work. Shaughnessy and Goulding use very practical examples to show us how self-organising, empowered teams can go about co-designing the best way to get work done. Innovation becomes Flow, the enterprise becomes agile.

— **Peter Hinssen, CO-founder Nexxworks and Author of *The Day After Tomorrow***

Goulding and Shaughnessy provide a method to move from doing digital to being digital. They have identified the shortcomings of the industrial era model and have developed an inspiring philosophy that blends people, process and innovation in a manner that will have people nothing short of rushing to work each day. They recognise that work in the digital age is essentially a form of self-expression directed towards the condition of the customer. *Flow* is more than a philosophy, it is a practical methodology designed to engage all stakeholders, and to ultimately harness the full cognitive capacity of the organisation's people. This is compulsory reading for business leaders.

**— Ade McCormack, International CIO,
Advisor and Speaker**

Flow is the perfect introduction to Business & Technical agility for those who are new to the field. It is smart/intuitive challenge to those readers who see themselves as experts. At its core it redefines how we go about digital transformation and create the new agile business.

— Serena de Stacpoole, Innovation Lead, Aviva

It's not often that I pick up a book and say "Those guys can talk the talk and walk the walk"! In *Flow* you get a common sense blueprint for doing an Agile Transformation from scratch, out of the box and in a very visual format. Buy this book, learn from this book and then start experimenting in your organisation. This will give you better communication, visibility of work and also keep you focused on the human factors in your Agile Transformations.

— Scott Sievwright, Agile Coach, Royal Bank of Scotland

Fantastic insight into Flow principles using real examples. A step into the future in a wonderfully presented book.

— Amazon review

Another great set of tools for the CIO/DTO toolbox. I'm a big fan of the "Wall" concept, as it promotes a high degree of collaboration and awareness without the technology getting in the way.

— Abe McIntosh, Digital transformation leader.

I couldn't have developed Flow without the love,
guidance and input from my wife Eugenia Mantero,
for which I'll be eternally grateful.

Fin

To Sip and Sophia and married bliss.

Haydn

ACKNOWLEDGEMENTS

We have been given encouragement and support from many people whose opinions we value throughout the development of this book. We'd like to give them a shout out, with the usual proviso that we are responsible for all errors and omissions. Seamus Keogan and David McGrath at SQS in Dublin have been immensely helpful and encouraging, while MD Phil Codd's generous support has allowed us to to take advantage of their time. Sean Twomey at Paddy Power Betfair gave us a great steer on the origins of Flow as well as providing wisdom on new units of work. His colleague Alan Murphy was a font of knowledge on testing. At Aviva, Serena de Stacpoole has supported us energetically and with invaluable insights on the work expectations of young people. Niall Moran exposed our weaknesses on user experience and worked hard to put us on the right track. Gwenn Clayton has been a cheerleader for us and provided vision for what Flow could be. Catherine Wilson helped with marketing. Special thanks to Gene Kim (author of the Phoenix Project) for his guidance too. Jim Dolce at FujiFilm North America has been a great enthusiast whose support we have valued deeply. Ade McCormack and Abe McIntosh have validated the approach from the perspective of two experienced CIOs. Thanks also to Jenn Sertl for support and for giving us an audience for Flow in Rochester, NY. Brian Shoenbaum and Chelsea Collier's enthusiasm in Austin also showed us the concepts can travel a long way. Anna Jarvis, as ever, has provided superb design support. Mary Walshe was not just a reader but a provider of valuable insight into personal development in the modern workplace. Fionnuala Conaty generously shared ideas about her own personal development goals. Ciaran O'Leary at SQS helped us understand more of the pedagogic journey people need to take with new ideas. Shiloh Schroeder and Rachel Langaker at Fusion Creative served us well on layout.

CONTENTS

INTRODUCTION

The Value-Seeking Enterprise

Welcome to a book that gives you with a step by step guide to becoming an agile business, one full of innovation, staffed by people whose passion is to seek value.

After a decade of pretending to empower people or to flatten the hierarchy and build collaboration, the moment of truth has arrived. The future belongs to enterprises that can create a value-seeking culture where people interact constructively, imaginatively and respectfully to uncover and meet customer needs through continuous innovation.

The problem with this scenario is how elusive it can be. That hit home for us while sitting in the boardroom of a major institution in London's financial district a couple of years back. It was an untypically warm day and the room, bordered by high glass windows, was stifling. This organisation had committed itself to transformation. Yet every person sat at that table, dressed in immaculate suits, had a conflicting objective. How to protect his own turf (yes, they were all men). The tension in the air stemmed from one thing only, apart from the heat. The communal resistance to change.

They graciously accepted every suggestion we, in this case Haydn, made about how to design projects that would allow teams to break with the past. They made a promise to look at the proposals closely over the coming weeks. But there was an inevitability about the lack of action that would follow. It's an experience familiar to Fin too whose work at multiple high performing companies has demonstrated time and again that fear and conflict at the top holds back huge amounts of potential.

On that particular day in London, Haydn was again looking at months of wasted work. In different places up and down the hierarchy, smart people knew what had to change. Plenty of people read about success and witness it all around them. They grow an instinct for what will work or at the very least for what will work better. They know where many of the problems lie in their company. What can possibly get senior people to feel at ease with empowering these people? As we move towards enterprises that are more of a network of relationships than a formal hierarchy, how do we make available the support structures that are a normal part of relationship building: trust, pleasure, enthusiasm, satisfaction?

Many companies have now hired digital transformation officers to overcome resistance to change. Our experience is that Chief Digital Transformation Officers can also be at a loss. They need a framework and practical tools to help them change work patterns and corporate culture. What this framework might be has obsessed both of us as we have observed resistance, conflict and wasted opportunity.

The challenge is that while worklife was defined by logic, process, carefully planned workflow, well defined roles and handover points, it is now defined by relationships and emotions. In many cases, especially for senior people, the prevailing emotion can be fear; primarily the fear of losing position, income and opportunity if the company begins to create wealth in ways that are not dependent on hierarchy. That fear and distrust can permeate corporate culture. At that point, the network of relationship that make up the real power base of the firm simmers with low-level toxicity.

When we, Fin and Haydn, discuss this problem we come back to the same answer. We need a way to reassert positive emotions as change takes place. We need people to have a burning passion for going into work, even as the workplace becomes more uncertain. The sense of risk that goes with uncertainty has to be a compelling reason to be in work. We need a framework where people will go out of their way to create value. The mid-to-large size enterprise has to feel like a startup full of people with ideas about what comes next.

We have been working on that challenge for some years. What is needed, we both realised, is a focus on people and how they interact. The business networks and relationships that make for agility are underpinned by good social interaction. Business consultants advise on issues like collaboration, community and social business platforms. But in the end, what companies lack are the venues and focal points for good social interaction and powerful relationship building. Of course, that is not divorced from good work and successful outcomes. The two go hand-in-glove. Interacting well and succeeding feed off each other. Agility is about using these patterns of good social interaction to allow people to codesign a new way of work for themselves.

The ability and power for colleagues to codesign the right process for any given set of tasks is a good definition for agility. All other methods and frameworks are really attempts to avoid empowering people. They are ways to stop people being the authors of their own "new ways to work". Responsible management means having a framework that guides and supports staff to do good codesign. Empowerment means letting them get on with it.

So what are the practical steps for getting there? That's what this book is all about. 12 practical steps to transformation, designed for everyone with an interest in new ways to work. In this book we are focused on frameworks that create true agility. We have defined a light framework for a new kind of social interaction, one where people become value-seeking, and one where leaders can feel assured that empowerment is not a threat.

We believe the framework we will outline (and began in *Flow: A Handbook For Change-Makers*) is the best way to create business agility. To truly empower people, you have to strip away old rules and processes and rely on employees to create new ones. To guide them you need a framework for focusing them on true value. We will take you through the major steps you need to achieve that, beginning with how to think in new ways about customers and ending with a view on how this feeds into big strategy. In the middle we will talk about new ways to work.

There are various aspects of our viewpoint that traditionalists probably disagree with. For example we believe that wealth creation will be characterised by many more units of work (we explain units of work later) engaged in exponentially more innovation. These will be designed by the people who execute them. The group will be the leader. Work will take place in highly visual and much more social environments. And people will be surrounded by critical non-essentials, or support mechanisms, that will be less about rules and more about emotions and relationship building. It will be leadership by social interaction.

THE INFLUENCE OF MATRIX INNOVATION

The expansion of innovation is a natural outcome of being networked with customers. Beginning with the World Wide Web, companies have had the opportunity to address much broader audiences with more and more products. The Web is essentially a global catalogue and people are demonstrably looking to satisfy a wide variety of needs. They mix ultra-niche purchases with mass-market products.

At the same time, the capabilities of IT have been evolving such that it is now possible to satisfy those broader segments cost effectively. Business platforms or online markets (see Chapter 12) have evolved to help further.

Here is an example. When someone bought a mobile phone in 2000, they had a small number of preinstalled apps and access to game downloads through sites like Handango. By and large, the purpose of the download was to generate revenues for the mobile network. Though the game market was developing quickly, the business model was to burn minutes of mobile network time.

When someone bought an iPhone in 2010 they were able to choose from hundreds of thousands of apps that they could download and use on the device. The emphasis in the revenue model switched from satisfying the needs of large network providers to providing opportunity for app developers and device makers. But the most interesting behavioural change lay with consumers. They were suddenly able to customise their total experience of the phone by creating a unique combination of functionality through their apps. App icons on the homescreen, in effect, represented each customer's unique version of the iPhone.

A similar change had been taking place on ecommerce sites like Amazon and eBay. People were able to meet a wider range of their needs and satisfy more of their interests. This phenomenon became known as the long-tail.

The long-tail is combination of individual interests and needs that people are out to satisfy. Very often it consists of many thousands of small markets that previously could not be served cost-effectively. Apple's IoS and Google's Android are designed to serve long-tail markets. Companies like Amazon are set up to serve the long-tail in physical goods.

More organisations need to address long-tail needs. The capabilities of IT now let's this happen. The advent of new techniques like microservices and emergent architectures mean that companies can create many new products, functionalities and services without having to adapt the digital infrastructure of the firm.

However, many managers were brought up to believe in a single identity for their companies, a single operational model, and a very limited range of products for mass-market customer segments. This is the old product innovation model. It is outdated. We are now in matrix innovation mode. Digital transformation requires leaders move to a matrix innovation mentality where they address hundreds or thousands of market segments with innovation everyday.

In the context of a matrix, new types of workflow emerge. Small incremental steps, yielding marginal gains, supported by what we refer to as critical *non-essentials* become more important, as do tools such as microservices, and the techniques we promote in Flow: value-seeking behaviour, asset discovery, work codesign, and small units of work visually represented to create a continuous dialogue about value.

CRITICAL NON-ESSENTIALS AND MARGINAL GAINS

Flow is a framework where people design their own work processes, in very visual environments and with huge amounts of social interaction.

Flow, at its heart, echoes many business theories, not least those that say action and everyday decision making are more important than big strategies. Some of the incrementalism we aim for resonates with older business books such as the 1980s classic *In Search of Excellence*. However, we do not search for excellence. Excellence can kill off companies, indeed whole industries (see Chapter 6). We search for value. We do that in the context of continuous improvement. To do this we need new tools.

Traditionally, work consisted of things you could see, critique and discuss. You could pick up tricks and tips from colleagues who had done something similar before. You were on display so you upped your game. You could inquire of colleagues or even get hit with advice you did not want.

Ironically, the digital environment has taken us through a revolution where social interaction and visibility have declined. Most work is now hidden in laptops or buried in reports. Our view of visibility and interaction is they have to be reintroduced during digital transformation. We use a lot of visualisation in Flow, as you will see in our first book. But since we wrote it we have also been contemplating how new ideas from other fields fit into Flow.

In the 12 Steps we draw on concepts from sport: critical non-essentials and marginal gains. Critical Non-essentials is clearly a paradoxical term but it means, simply, that some parts of our processes can appear non-essential yet can be critical to success. This is particularly true of work culture.

Clive Woodward, who coached the England Rugby World Cup team to victory in 2003, talked about these Critical Non-essentials as central to the team ethos. It was not muscle mass, speed or the structural plays of the English team that won the World Cup. Each of these is necessary and without them you are not a contender. However, the non-essentials were less obvious. He insisted that people be 10 minutes early for meetings to show respect for each other. Changing shirts at halftime to reset the mind for the rest of the game to come had a marginal effect too. The development of rapid eye movement and practising decision making under pressure, added more marginal gains.

Those ideas were taken up by the British cycling squad that went on to take record hauls at the London Olympics and was taken on too by Team Sky. The cycling team aimed to do 100 things 1% better. That meant the team, embracing coaches and riders, went in search of all the marginal gains available to them, including avoiding the struggle to be competitive in non-Olympic events. Their focus was total.

Marginal gains signifies the whole team's potential to create many small improvements that add up to something very big. The whole team is not just the players. Marginal gains have to be sought by coaches, physios, medics, and even bus drivers.

We use these two terms to explain what we think happens within Flow and matrix-innovation. Marginal gains become central to designing the organisation around smaller units of work and maximising benefit from them. We think of Critical Non-essentials when we think of Appreciation Walls or Job Walls. Not at all essential, on the face of things, but critical to success.

Increasingly, those characteristics we thought we could exclude from work, such emotion and caring, are being shown to be critical. You cannot have networks of relationships unless you care and in Flow we have visual ways to show appreciation and support. They are particularly important when innovation becomes more matrix-like.

THE NEED FOR A VALUE-SEEKING CULTURE IN AN AGILE BUSINESS

In matrix-innovation there is so much new going on that it is easy to be seduced by novelty for its own sake. In place of "just-innovating" or stalling work in order to make complex ROI calculations or just getting on with the next project, we need to foster a culture of intelligent conversations about where value lies. This is value-seeking behaviour.

Innovation is becoming multi-tiered, multi-faceted and fast. Good firms create innovation in a continuous flow of new initiatives, features and strategic responses. They innovate dozens of times a day and are responsive to consumer reactions to their products and services. These are features of agile businesses.

Value-seeking behaviour is a discipline that shapes the way teams function. In place of fulfilling roles and completing projects that might have no value, employees are encouraged to seek value at every turn, in every segment, in every task-breakdown and at every reflection point.

There is a bigger issue behind why this is necessary. Innovation now has to contend with multiple system changes in the wider economy. The emerging economic landscape includes: Autonomous cars, blockchain, private cryptocurrencies, the Internet of Things, AI, robotics, virtual reality, digital processes, business platforms and huge scale where companies have billions of customers. The future is marked by profound system change: The ability to match internal capabilities with this multi-layered, systemic transformation, and ally them to the right enterprise structure, represents a huge new challenge.

Creating the culture to respond to all of this will define future success. These system changes impose extraordinary demands on organisations to do things better and faster. There are very few tried and tested routes to success when everything is so new. Making the right choices from dozens of new possibilities, everyday, will be an outcome of value-centric behaviour rather than following the rules. Behaviour replaces process.

Flow fosters a number of necessary behavioural characteristics that go a long way to enabling the right responses to rapid change. It emphasises the power of intelligent interaction over conformity. Flow also involves:

- A different way of seeing customers where we strive for real customer-centricity.

- The willingness to disrupt the normal cadence of work.

- Being adaptive about business goals.

- Using extensive visualisation of work to create venues for interaction.

- Creating a culture of process codesign so that people own new processes.

- Creating a framework to promote value-seeking behaviour through better social interaction and critical non-essentials.

- Taking small steps towards new strategies.

Where we have implemented these ideas or where we have seen them grow organically, our experience is that they define a new agility and a better way to work.

INTRODUCING THE FLOW VALUE STACK

Because the customer-base of any company is now infinitely varied, enterprises succeed when they innovate constantly over multiple product and service segments. They are attempting to deliver more value every day, often in situations where the very structures of an industry are changing (what we call systemic innovation or phase-change).

This introduces the need for that new cadence of work. Stuff has to get done faster and better. And it can be done. Technology systems allow us to innovate hundreds of times a day. To take advantage of that though, we need a new culture that puts value first; before ego-projects, before hierarchy and before existing work routines and rules.

There are of course older definitions of value in business. Most of them stem from the Value Management movement, introduced in the 1940s at GE. Value Management recognises that any initiative will involve a balance between stakeholder needs and resources spent.

There is also a very substantial body of thought around value-stream mapping (or analysing processes to remove wasted effort). Value-stream mapping is often referred to as a way to reach a future state from where a set of processes stand today. It is an in depth analysis of how to get work done more efficiently.

There is a clear overlap between these two. The latter is more cost-driven whereas the former maintains a conscious view of the ultimate reward - customer satisfaction - at a reasonable cost. However, both are methods that disguise the core problem of all work. How do we know when we are creating value?

This is where the people factor comes in again. There is something fundamentally subjective about this. Once you introduce the idea of customer value or customer satisfaction, you also introduce subjective judgments about how much energy and cost should go into creating it or indeed whether that value will be appreciated and paid for. You introduce risk. You can plan to create value only for customers to reject you. You can do great projects that lead to no value. You can be on time and on budget and your products or services can still stink.

Value-stream mapping and value management can help you to feel like you are on the right track, but there are doubts over whether they make a positive contribution to customer success. We need new tools that shape and direct all the extra judgments that we now have to make. We cannot afford to get lost in reports and analyses.

Flow promotes the ideal of value-seeking behaviour. If you do not understand value-seeking culture then chances are your teams will be doing good work according to the rules and processes you have laid out for them. But it is very hard to say that they are doing valuable work just because they follow rules.

Being agile, however, is about human interaction. All culture is really about interaction rather than rules. As well as creating rigid processes, many enterprises reduce the scope of human interaction and create workflow conflicts. That's another way of saying, they kill good culture, often because they haven't understood how to respond to what is emerging around them. There is no magic pill or solution to the challenge of creating a good culture. There is no software solution, though plenty of companies have put their faith in software platforms. The only answer is to create good social interaction and to direct it towards value-seeking behaviour.

To build a culture around value-seeking behaviour we introduced the Flow Value Stack.

The Flow Value Stack

1. Segmentation and customer success analysis

2. Agile Portfolios

3. Flexible business goals

4. Continuous value hypotheses

5. Disrupting the cadence of work
(as well as delivering, testing, iterating)

6. Customer Feedback Walls

7. Flow value optimisation reviews

We'll go into more detail later. In fact, much of the book will be about the detail! But here is a brief summary:

Companies need to do more to understand their market segments. It is only by understanding long-tail segments that you can address unmet or emerging needs. Equally, they need to understand what success looks like for customers.

This is a first step towards creating work of value. However, it will make little impact if executive decision making overlooks these factors. That's why we work with Agile Portfolio Walls (like the Executive Portfolio Wall), to ensure that work is meeting the company's objectives.

The third feature in the value stack is the introduction of flexibility in business goals. Business goals traditionally have been used to specify requirements that get handed to IT as work-to-be-done. We need to introduce flexibility into this and allow developers to raise questions that might shift business goals. In addition we should ensure that goals (or outcomes) drive work design at all levels of the organisation. Goals not projects. When goals are flexible, different departments can interact constructively around value instead of simply attempting to meet a requirement.

Flexible goals imply a high level of hypothesis building. When you are breaking work down into smaller units (see next point) the purpose is to ensure that each discrete piece of work has value. Empowering people to question the value of work is an important cultural step.

Creating a new cadence of work involves disrupting accepted ideas about how long work should take. It also involves creating a very short cycle-time (how long it takes to get a unit of work done). That way everyone is interacting at least every second day, ideally more often. Within that faster cadence, work can be tested for value more frequently and changes can be made to goals or outputs at short notice. That test mentality is an interesting one. Tests can replace plans!

The next contribution to value is the Customer Feedback Wall, where all sources of data on user reactions to products, features and services are logged and dealt with transparently.

Finally, there is a value optimisation review or analysis; a periodic review of what is working and what is not.

While these points do not make up the structure of the book, we will come back to them throughout the discussions that follow.

WHAT YOU WILL GET FROM THIS BOOK

Businesses have spent a fortune in recent years avoiding good social interaction. Creating social business platforms, utilising streams, enterprise-type Facebook's etc., all act as an excuse not to engage in the most important aspect of work: encouraging and supporting more intense social interaction that is authentic and emotional.

We are aware that good social interaction at scale is difficult and there is a temptation to surround it with rules. Scrum agile gives you rules. Project management gives you rules. We have to acknowledge that people like to be somewhat bound by rules.

Smart people interacting creatively will also create rules. They create the right rules and the right processes for the job in hand. What they need is a framework that guides their social interaction.

That's why we have written this new book and why we are partnering with people to set up Flow Academies and practical training programs.

Moving on to new ways to work takes time, skill and reassurance. The most difficult concept for managers to accept is that this social interaction involves us in emotions. Rules, logic, analysis, and data are all ways to avoid emotion. But to interact more effectively we have to embrace emotion as a powerful force in wealth creation. Against that backdrop, these are the main lessons we want you to take from this book.

- Being able to design new ways to work.

- Knowing how to become truly agile across the whole business.

- Being comfortable with fewer rules and set structures.

- Creating real customer-centricity.

- Creating a value-seeking culture.

- Growing emotional resilience to support work in uncertainty.

- Being able to advocate a more effective approach to strategy.

We have put together 12 steps to heaven to accompany our illustrated book Flow. For best results read both.

CHAPTER 1

Talking About Business Agility: Using Flow Circles To Get You Started

We need to redesign change. We need new concepts for what change means. We need to be clear about the end goals of transformation. In fact, we need for people to codesign the changes they face. You cannot get away with phoney empowerment anymore.

We work with companies that routinely try to reorganise themselves without giving power away. It's often an annual ritual. Leaders facing market challenges decide to tinker with reporting lines and responsibilities. A few senior people get new titles, more or less responsibility and extra "direct reports". Organisations do this rather than face the need for a fundamental shift in their work cadence, work design and roles. But the tinkering deflates people's expectations of change. It creates insurmountable problems during digital transformation. People react by rejecting it.

Pretending to hand over the reins to people only to weigh them down with rules or have that reorg hanging over their heads is no longer an option. People have been there already.

In Flow, our aim is to create a dialogue so people get to define the change they are experiencing. That is not just cool. It is pragmatic. It is how a truthful person would define empowerment.

Empowerment means giving away power! If we can be honest about this we can start a movement.

Flow hands over power to people to redesign work, to make work more appropriate for the needs of the day, codesigning it to redirect their energy towards creating value instead of wasting time. Given the right framework they will be the co-authors of their own very positive change story. They will unlock their own talents.

As we said in the introduction, we wanted to find a way to achieve this without threatening leadership. Flow's value-seeking framework benefits everyone.

BASIC FLOW PRINCIPLES

Flow is a framework for business agility. Many other frameworks set rules and specify roles. They lock behaviour into rigid patterns. We prefer to think of the framework as a philosophy that people can embrace because it guides their interaction and focus, not because it rules them. Flow is not even our philosophy. It has grown out of authentic empowerment.

To understand it ask the question: If people are truly empowered, how would they act? The answer is that work would become far more social. Decisions would flow from the social interaction of smart people empowered to design the best way to reach new solutions.

In future, the enterprise will rely more on these networks of relationships rather than on tried and trusted processes and rules. By extension, the more we communicate with each other, especially about value, the better our decisions will be. There is something transparently, simplistically true about this and it relates to what we said in the introduction. Firms need to liberate people to have intelligent conversations focused on value. If you have poor relationships and poor communications, then the fortune of the firm rests with a few leaders and their superhuman powers. Good luck with that one! We've all seen it in action, leaders sweating in plush meeting rooms, fearful of their inability to make the next constructive move. Good designs, good development, authentic relationships and good decisions really come down to how people interact with each other. And leaders also need to be liberated from the expectations that have grown up around them.

To support better social communications up and down the hierarchy and across business functions, we use a number of "tools." They are not software tools. Our tools are methods to support relationships. They are built on the idea of value-seeking behaviour. To fully grasp Flow you will need to read our first Handbook, but we can summarise some points here.

- We visualise all work processes on the walls of the building (there are plenty of examples in the first book and a few schematics later in this chapter).

- Those work processes are designed by the people doing the work.

- Work is always designed around goals (business outcomes) but everybody has the right to challenge the value of the goal (a way of countering rigidity and disengagement when experience shows a goal is not creating value). In other words, they are designed around flexible business goals.

- We seek units of work that are 1-2 day chunks so people can get together more often to discuss outputs of their work and to assess its value.

- We have methods for becoming more customer-centric and having customer concerns drive innovation.

- We are also driven by the idea of value and customer success. Some of our methods create a focus on value-seeking behaviour and we believe that is a good philosophy for all work (and also for life!)

Flow could be described as a combination of Agile, lean principles and Kanban with a new value philosophy and customer-centricity thrown in. It becomes more than that because you are in control. You define work processes and you define your version of Flow. We urge people not to get caught up in the search for rules. Other people come up with new ways of applying Flow and so can you.

There are additional factors that become obvious once you are a practitioner.

- Thinking outside the project, being expressly anti-project management and collectively designing work so that value becomes clear (value, value, value).

- Minimising the drag-impact of budgeting, planning, scheduling and reporting. These things can be done quickly and incrementally so don't let people walk away to "write up the results of the meeting" (take photos instead).

- Promoting continuous learning.

- Creating emotional resilience. Change is allowing emotion back into the workplace. People need to design their personal development goals in order to become better practitioners of real time work design. It can be a scary ride but the future belongs to people with the emotional resilience to work in uncertain environments.

Taken together, these give you an entirely new approach to work. Flow Circles are a way for people to shape this transformation. Hosting Flow Circles is an acknowledgement that the change is for real this time round. It is not a reorg. Change will be directed by the people responsible for executing the work.

A Circle should be an environment where people speak freely about what matters to them. And that often means blockers! What blocks value? People go to work for a reason. As well as the pay cheque, they want to be involved in creating value. Value arises from creative acts. Situations, processes and people that block value are irksome to everyone. We are going to solve that problem. We will suggest ways to introduce venues for debating the events, people or cultures that are blocking change and how these can be disrupted and replaced by Flow. But first you may want to experiment a little.

EXPERIMENTING WITH FLOW

To begin a Flow implementation you can experiment with the Walls we outline in our first book. These are large scale visualisations of all work processes. Yes, literally. Decorate the Walls with visualisations of strategic direction, Customer Segmentation maps, major goals, work in progress, work allocation, Customer Feedback, upcoming job opportunities, job swaps, thank you messages, risks and issues, learning and academy time. Please take a look at the Handbook. Almost every chapter has a Wall; Chapter 6 lists a few that we've experimented and succeeded with, while Chapter 5 has a detailed account of the Executive Portfolio Wall.

Inevitably doing something different draws attention. Yet, Flow is becoming more widely used and the framework is flexible enough for you to adapt it. There is no reason to fear failure. Quite the opposite. Prepare to be creative. Be brave. Start with a focus on customer relationships (Customer Walls) and executive accountability (the Executive Portfolio Wall). We use customer walls, in particular, for:

- Customer-centric innovation.

- Customer feedback.

- Customer insights.

Many companies talk about customer-centricity without doing a whole lot to nail it down (more likely a senior executive will have

fired up a big data project and your customer-centricity journey will
be pushed years into the future).

Nonetheless, setting up simple walls that visualise the customer(s)
is a way to get immediate value from Flow. Set up a simple Customer
Feedback Wall in the entrance to your building (see Chapter 10 of
this book for a detailed Customer Feedback Wall). Take overnight
social media activity or call centre enquiries and post customer reactions on the Wall for everyone to see. Just record them on tweet
length statements on cards or Post-Its.

Design the Wall so that you see the latest feedback (backlog)
on the left of the diagram below, the start of the customer feedback
journey; prioritise it (column 2), and indicate to where it has been
referred. After a week, take a look at the Wall with a small group
of colleagues. What do you see? Where are the pain points most
concentrated? Where are the big issues being referred to? Add in
some photos, tweets from specific customers, reviews from websites.
Make it live.

A simple Customer Feedback Wall

Backlog of pain points	Prioritised backlog	Refer to digital team	Refer to marketing	Refer to logistics
☐ ☐ ☐	☐ ☐ ■	☐ ☐	☐ ☐	☐
DONE		☐ ☐		☐ ■ ☐

■ Big issue   ☐ Medium   ☐ Small

The Wall is a demonstration that you have your eye on what
customers are saying; you have it documented, you have a visual
representation of the scale of complaints, where these are being

referred to, and what is resolved. It's just a start, but Flow is all about taking small steps. It is also a good start because it makes customer-centricity real. It is good because their pain-points are instantly visible in a public place. When you create transparency, the effect will be to draw colleagues in. They will ask questions about the Wall and want to discuss shortcomings they've noticed too. A conversation has begun.

There is no specific template for Feedback Walls. What we suggest above is one way but not the way. Try it and see. Over time you can evolve the Customer Feedback Wall into a key component of your overall approach to value, as described in Chapter 10 (where we also look at how the Feedback Wall plays into process redesign and strategy). But to start with, think of just posting overnight enquiries, complaints, Facebook comments or tweets. You can share this experience in an early Flow Circle. But suppose your first action is to discuss issues rather than to initiate a Wall. What might the conversation look like?

BEGINNING THE MOVEMENT

Culture is central to value creation. By inference, so too is social interaction. If you cannot interact constructively then there will be few benefits of digital work. So what is blocking good social interaction (the other way of saying culture)? That becomes a critical question when you are planning a Flow Circle.

A Flow Circle is not just a meeting. It is a commitment to building a meeting of minds. You know you need change. Are you going to wait forever? Or are you going to generate aspects of good culture that you and your colleagues can then help to spread? Will you wait for empowerment or show how beneficial empowerment can be?

A Flow Circle is a place to create empowerment as a responsible movement focused on value.

The meeting of minds should zone in on good social interaction. You cannot have a good, constructive culture without strong social interaction. The two are synonymous. Business agility is only possible when you remove impediments to strong interaction, though many work environments are sometimes openly and sometimes subtly the opposite.

So what is blocking good, appropriate work? Very often it can be traced back to a lack of communication, over-formal communications (meetings!!), communication that is one way (rules or dominant egos), or simply a lack of understanding. It may sound naive. Can high performance really come down to good social interaction? 'Fraid so!

Blockers can also be things like leadership culture, unexpected demands on time, scrum masters who are treating sprints like currency, interdepartmental resentments or frequent misalignments such as merging the work of different teams and finding they don't quite fit. Meetings too are a blocker, if your aim is value. All the evidence shows that the majority of meetings are unproductive so what can replace them? Wall visualisations!

The objective when raising these issues in a Circle is not to moan or point the finger. It's something else. If you can't find a forum for being honest about your struggles, what hope is there of moving past them? Let's be more emphatic about that. You cannot create a movement that empowers a group of like-minded people if you are dishonest.

A Flow Circle can help get blockers out into the open - chalk them up on your first Flow Wall. Here are some important considerations.

A FEW PREREQUISITES FOR FLOW AS A MOVEMENT.

1. **Be sure to understand Flow first.** Flow is not a set of rules or a rigid methodology. It is a way to create more social interaction around value and to promote value-seeking behaviour. The principle techniques are the Wall Visualisations and reduced cycle-time. The latter is a way to say "getting work done faster." Reducing cycle-time disrupts the normal cadence of work. Giving up on the idea of projects and instead thinking of small units of work frees you to have conversations that all other methods inhibit. Those conversations give you a caucus for all kinds of agreements around just-in-time work process design and just-in-time testing. These methods lead people to create ways of work that are appropriate for the task or problem at hand (instead of following rules). Try to get these concepts into your own mind before hosting a group. Moving away from rules-based behaviour to value-seeking behaviour appears to be difficult. Surprisingly, it often comes naturally. People just need to know this is for real.

2. **Clarify your goals visually and iterate.** Is there a specific set of goals that you believe needs addressing or developing? In Flow we try to be sure all work is driving towards an outcome or goal. In general, we also try to visualise that. Consider having a Wall outline ready, so you can begin to log goals and any actions that stem from the discussion (the Post-Its below the goals in the table below represent actions). You don't have to go this far but think about it. Make it your Pilot Wall.

A simple Wall for setting goals for a Flow Circle

Goals →

Identifying blockers	Resolving resource issues	Raising authenticity, e.g. in customer first goal	Improving personal development	Conflict management	

■ Large problem   ▢ Medium   ▢ Small

3.   **Be transparent** - advertise the Circle on a board, in internal newsletters and in online conversations. However you phrase it, what are you actually saying? We want to take our own initiatives in becoming more agile. We believe this is the way to be empowered rather than waiting for permission. Who is interested? That seems to us a pretty mature view of your responsibilities.

4.   **Be empowered** - to be empowered is to take responsibility. Stop waiting around for other people to do it.

5.   **Link Flow to new initiatives.** Often, elements of Flow are introduced when there is a new body of work to get done (like a Cloud migration or a new set of product features for a website). By linking Flow to a new product or initiative, it is easier to say, "we need new ways to work: who wants to look at new tools for business agility?" Flow does not have to be linked to new initiatives. It can be its own initiative, especially as a way to bring marketing and IT together.

6. **Invite people with different skill sets** - team leaders, new hires and senior leaders who will all have or aspire to a leadership role. Include business analysts who have to face the challenge of renewing their work breakdown skills, marketers who need to rethink customer segmentation; people who have a specific profile and who get the fact that the company has fundamental issues with an untrusting culture.

7. **Invite people in digital transformation roles.** If you leave out people with an obvious stake in change methods you will run into opposition later. Flow is not a shadow activity. It is important both to stress too that Flow needs to start with small steps. It is a ground-up initiative.

8. **Keep the C-Suite appraised.** Any significant new work in a company will have to find C-Suite backing sooner or later. There is value in sending an invite to a CIO, CMO or a CXO with the proviso that this is just a starter discussion. Maybe the CIO can start things off?

9. **It's the whole business** - Flow is not a special set of rules for IT. It is a framework for the whole business. Don't forget that.

SETTING THE SCENE FOR OTHER PEOPLE

In our first Flow Circles we make it a rule to allow people to stop being polite and to raise real issues (for details to support your first Flow leadership meeting see *Flow: A Handbook....*). However, we also set a few ground rules:

1. *Raising only professional issues* - the discussion is about the issue or the problem not about the person. Take per-

sonal politics out of every discussion. ***It's professional, not personal.***

2.   ***The meeting has equal share of voice*** - nobody should expect to sit, listen and absorb, without contributing. Equally nobody should dominate; nor should it become a meeting where a coterie of people can claim special insight; we all start from scratch. There are no Flow experts because all Flow techniques are open to redesign.

3.   ***Empathetic leadership*** - Leaders need to orchestrate and ***generate belief*** - here's an opportunity to practice that critical skill by being inclusive. It's worth also giving younger people responsibility for Flow. It's a movement for change, after all.

4.   ***Flow Circles really need to drive towards technique*** - you have blockers and issues and work going wrong. You have to drive towards solutions. You have to identify the problems honestly and move onto a conversation about how Flow techniques will help solve them. We think about the visualisation of small steps towards an answer, with regular conversations about the breakdown of the journey. As you identify problems, your next step is to say: What small steps can we take? Maybe Step 1 is that Goals Wall above.

5.   ***Everybody should say why they are at the meeting*** - open up about your marvellous array of hidden or not so obvious skills. Emphasise not so much what do people want to get out of meeting but what do they have to contribute to rethinking work? What skill, reading, insight, tools, tricks, workarounds and experiences have they in their personal locker that they've been keen to explore in work but have not been able to. What can the Circle, or Flow, liberate for them?

PROVIDING INFORMATION ON THE "WHY!"

It is important to be upfront about why new ways of work are necessary. It is constructive to openly discuss the limitations of existing techniques and what is replacing them. As most of your non-technical colleagues will have very little grasp of how IT is changing and making new things possible, they need to be informed.

Many companies have invested heavily in Scrum Agile or Scaled Agile Frameworks. If these work for you then fine. Don't break what works. But in many cases those frameworks are rigid and are not easy to apply across the business. Neither Agile nor Lean Startup is well adapted to the realities of medium to large enterprises in today's economy. Yes, a decade back they were good. But today is different. Introduce non-technical colleagues to the why by looking at:

1.　Microservices

2.　The broader trend to smaller work packages

3.　DevOps

4.　The new competitive environment

1.　Microservices is a new software architecture that disaggregates software into smaller packages. It opens up the possibility of large companies innovating more often without those innovations having a disruptive impact on the overall architecture. Along with DevOps they allow you to act like a startup, regardless of size. Agile methods are too long-winded to maximise the agility unleashed by microservices and DevOps.

2.　The trend to small is widespread: more relationships with smaller companies, smaller market niches in the long-tail, microservices and micro-apps and smaller units of work. In this environment it becomes essential to do more and do it quickly whilst forever focusing on what is of value. Agile does not have the tools for this type of value-seeking behaviour.

3.   *DevOps*, the combination of development, testing and operations into a single team allows for continuous delivery and integration. That means the work environment has to adapt to continuous innovation. It also points the way to true business agility: holistic teams that span the whole business.

4.   *The competitive environment* places more demands on us to ensure customers succeed with our products and services, even if this means constantly creating something new for them. The wider setting for that is the extreme nature of technical innovation; blockchain, digital currencies and the move to mobile wallets and cashless transactions; AI, autonomous vehicles; drones; the Internet of Things, and highly scaled competition from China. All of this is creating new levels of expectation as well as suggesting further industry convergence that will bring new competitors into every field of the economy. You need to be more agile than ever.

These can also be within your goals. You can start to document how you might respond to these challenges. You can sketch out the goals you might want to address in a Circle.

A simple Wall for setting goals

Goals ──▶

Informing the business about new capabilities re: microservices	Identifying risks, issues and responses to global competition	Creating broader participation in Devops teams	Engaging marketing in the analysis of smaller opportunities	Identifying blockers	Resolving resource issues
▢ ▢	▢ ▢ ▢	◼ ▢	▢ ▢	▢	◼ ▢ ▢

◼ Large problem   ▢ Medium   ▢ Small

CRITICAL QUESTIONS AND TOPICS

There are some critical questions you can introduce at an initial Flow Circle. We have already suggested major topics that will be impacting people (like Microservices and DevOps). And we have stressed the importance of opening up about blockers. Still, you want a positive agenda too.

PUT CUSTOMERS FIRST:

Ask, do we really have the customer's success at the heart of what we are doing? Is your work looping around customers the way it does in Flow? Very often, organisations are honing in on big data as a way to avoid real customer engagement. Data helps to cross-sell and upsell. It is good for micro-targeting. There's nothing wrong in sales expansion but it needs to be off the back of showing customers you can help meet their needs. So what small steps can you take towards this real form of customer-centricity? How can you ground customer-centricity in reality instead of sloganeering? How can you counter the company's tendency to keep falling short of authenticity on this?

CRITICAL NON-ESSENTIALS AND MARGINAL GAINS

We introduced these terms at the beginning of this book. We think it's a good idea to raise them in a Flow Circle. The examples we have given might not be the best for you. But looking around your office or team, what do you recognise as critical non-essentials or areas where you can make many marginal gains? Is there something in your geographic location, in relationship building, shared leisure interests, skills' pooling, time-keeping or learning that can give you many new but small advantages? They will become more obvious as you move to a different cadence of work and more visual interaction.

AGILE PORTFOLIOS AND EXECUTIVE DECISION MAKING

Very often Executive Portfolios lack agility. They can be ill-aligned with corporate goals and are rarely agile enough to capture changing customer needs. Being transparent about this is a good conversation. Executives often make portfolio decisions without direct input from dynamic customer segmentation. The Portfolio becomes static and a drag on your capacity to be responsive. Is this your problem?

WORK BREAKDOWN

Is your work breakdown and work allocation causing integration problems or creating dependencies that slow you down? Do projects live or die in reports? If so, can you try out a Wall for better work breakdown and try using photographs?

Use a Circle to do a project breakdown session just to test your skills at real time project description driven by the principle of supporting customer success and seeking value. You will find examples of customer segmentation and work breakdown for reduced cycle-time later in the book.

PERSONAL DEVELOPMENT

Towards the end of the book we talk about personal development and new roles. It's important to look at the way roles are changing. There are three aspects to it.

1. The first is to do with fungibility. We need people to be less rigid about role definitions and to be more multi-skilled. People need to gain more satisfaction from their capacity to perform various roles rather than to follow rules.

2. We need people to break with the traditional cadence of work. People need to get more pleasure out of working quicker, and ending the work-cycle with a real achievement. But doing that in an uncertain environment with less rules means they also need to know how to set personal boundaries and to grow their resilience.

3. We need to switch out of old agile roles, such as product owners and scrum masters, to something that reflects the new need for value management.

Many organisations do not invest in these changes but Wall Visualisations can be a small step to getting it underway.

IDEAS AND TESTING

How do you respond to new ideas in your culture? As teams, what's your instinctive reaction to a new idea or suggestion? Do you open up to the possibility or close it out? If you close it out then why? What would make you more open to talking about real possibilities rather than dismissing ideas as improbable?

BEGINNING

1. Create a short, visual document that says how you can work differently.

2. Create a Goals Wall for a Flow Circle.

3. Re-segment your customer base without analytics: make it a conversation.

4. Invite people from across the business to talk

CHAPTER 2

The Customer in the Agile Business

In this chapter we are going to concentrate on refreshing your customer segmentation, a topic we first raised in *Flow*. We will also look at customer success, a new concept developed in Software as a Service (SaaS) environments. Why bother?

1. There is a Chinese motto along the lines of every great journey begins with the first step. It's like saying: the path to glory is not made up of huge victories. We compose greatness from the small details. Business used to conceive of "customers" as a mass market, stimulated by mass advertising, coaxed into purchases by large companies with charismatic leaders and dominant brands. Today, heroic behaviour lies in the detail, the segments where people are composing their own special lives. Being agile boils down to how many of these segments you serve well enough to keep the competition at bay. Certainly without analysing segments you will not create information about upstream value and you will waste downstream resources.

2. The second issue is that people think of agility as a process advantage (being able to pivot to meet new needs) when,

in fact, it begins with a deeper appreciation of customers (why you ***need*** to pivot).

3.   A lot of value in organisations is lost or wasted because of a lack of insight upstream, before a product or services go into development. Projects flow downstream where the impetus is to complete them, while assuming that they have value simply because they have been funded and an argument in favour of them has already been won. If you are diligent about segmenting your customer base you can assess customers' unmet needs and define the best ways of meeting them. Dynamic customer segmentation is your best upstream value analysis tool.

4.   We want you to end this chapter thinking differently about customers, how you can enrich their lives by optimising the flow of innovation in your enterprise, and how that can become part of the daily conversation at work.

5.   We want you to recognise deeper knowledge of customer segments as the key to business agility and also to good resource allocation. Most executives have a sense of how big data will allow more precise targeting. However, agility is not about selling. The idea of agility is all about meeting more needs, at higher value, for a wider range of customers and that involves good upstream analysis.

6.   You need to move beyond the two main customer insight tools: big data, and simple personas or caricatures of customers, to rich segmentations where you can identify many, new emerging needs.

7.   This should provide you with a powerful platform for targeting your innovation efforts. You will target innova-

tion better. This will broaden the flow of innovation and raise the demands on people inside your company to work much smarter (by adopting many of the features of Flow).

Authentic customer-centricity is often a distant dream for companies, even the ones that espouse customer-centric philosophies. It is an easy language to adopt but there is some hard graft involved in the reality. It is also one where the emphasis is only half right. It is right to think about customers' downstream appreciation of your services. But you need to do the upstream work too. Get it right and your company will be a star innovator. It can also be a focal point bringing together different parts of the business. It can help bridge divides. It can give focus to innovation. It can be a strong discipline as you start to think of how to deliver value to different segments of your market.

Customer success on the other hand forces us to switch our mindset away from: "what will we get out of this?" to "how can we help customers create more successful experiences?"

Later in this chapter we will introduce a set of tools to help embed customer centricity and customer success. Say hello to **CATE:**

CUSTOMER SEGMENTATION, ASSET DISCOVERY, TARGETED IDEATION, AND ECOSYSTEM BUILDING.

First, though, a taster of poor customer segmentatIon from the car industry. We mentioned in our first book that lots of people do not go back to distributor garages once their car warranty ends. We also noted that the majority of decisions about cars are made by women, or influenced by them, and women are especially interested in maintaining their cars. They are absolutely the single most important part of the customer-base.

We asked around about their experiences at distributorships and received comments like:

1. Well if they wouldn't look you up and down the minute you walk in, it would be a whole lot better.

2. I got sold new brake shoes and didn't know if I needed them really (she didn't!).

3. It's almost impossible to get into work from there.

4. They start by asking me questions I don't know the answer to so I feel stupid the minute I walk in.

5. The last time I went to buy a car they kept trying to selling me finance.

These comments point to a number of success factors that might all come under the heading "Leaving happy."

1. Absence of sexual aggression.

2. Verifiable transparency.

3. Ease of access.

4. Empathetic selling.

5. Appropriate selling.

None of these are difficult to deliver but most car companies don't bother. They have their operational model and they have their big data projects. They will figure out a way to influence the sale rather than create a "leave happy" culture.

Before you read on, pause for a minute and log the instances of poor interaction you encounter as a customer each day. From commuting, to queuing at planes, to doctors and hospitals, to junk mail and electronic spam. Maybe it was a dud subscription you can't get rid of. What was your customer experience like, today? Do suppliers innovate for you?

WHY FIRMS FAIL WITH AGILITY - THE MATRIX INNOVATION PROBLEM

Much innovation literature is written for people developing new products for new customers. It is extraordinarily linear in nature. The obvious difference with established companies is they already provide many customers with a broad range of products or services. Much of the innovation they engage in concerns the update of existing products, or creating new features to enhance those products, or adding new products that are an addition to a product line. They are likely to be experiencing several kinds of disruption. One of these is the atomisation of customer demand. That's a way of saying more people want different things, more often. Markets are fragmenting. New segment demand is emerging all the time, changing the way upstream value is forming.

Take all these together and Normal Corp needs a broad matrix of innovation at different stages of maturity, along with new ways to think about value.

Doing good customer segmentation is an essential component of matrix innovation. A dynamic segmentation is the moat that prevents competitors swimming easily towards your customer base. But it also allows you to differentiate between nice to have and must-have innovation. To do this you need data but not big data. You need a *variety* of data sources allied to imagination, so you can draw and then redraw segments, through your everyday conversations.

Most companies possess numerous sources of information about customers, even if they don't use them intelligently. They will have installed bots in call-centres, which give them a stronger ability to analyse customer feedback in real-time. They have regular call-centre logs. They have access to social media listening. They should be experienced in search engine analytics. And they may have a big data project that is seeking out hidden patterns of demand.

The problem is that both IT and marketing think of customers as idealised or caricatured *personas*. This absolutely kills any chance of upstream value analysis. Personas are caricatures. They are make believe typologies of customers. Brian, a 35 year old carpenter whose income is increasing year on year and wears green jumpers. Julie, an empty nester who is figuring out how to rebalance her life.

Developers also use personas as they develop User Stories just as marketers use them to create campaigns. Personas are made up. It means the customer does not exist within the mind of the organisation that uses them.

These personas are a kind of segmentation but a weak one. They are too generalised and they are static. Companies that stop looking at real customers fail to spot changing needs, leading to the risk of disruption. Startups are quick onto those missed segment opportunities.

In our own work, we help companies to reach more and more complex segmentations as a prelude to appropriate and relevant innovation. Marcelle Speller, who co-founded the leading European holiday rentals site in the first decade of this century (holiday-rentals.com) told us that her segmentation amounted to about 5,000 categories. She was serving about 5.000 different customer types, or segments, and these categories would be shifting over time. So segmentation is extremely important. It is core to the long-tail economy we live in.

Can you avoid better segmentation if you have a big data project? You'd be crazy to confuse the two. Big data uncovers hidden patterns of demand you can sell to. It lets you micro-target audiences. It does not help you to innovate continuously. Although it can play a part in better segmentation, it is not a substitute for creative insights and dialogue. At the same time, simpler segmentations bind companies into rigid ideas about customers and, by extension, limit their insights into their innovation possibilities. These are all ways of saying that companies fail to address the upstream value problem.

EXAMPLE 1: FASHION AND BEAUTY

A good example of failed customer segmentation and lack of agility comes from the world of fashion and beauty. Fashion companies make their living by constantly innovating. They are not laggards. They shape taste. In the digital era, however, a number of new companies have been able to move into their space.

Over the past five years self-images for dating sites have created a new demand for digitally enhanced beauty. This is a very interesting development. In a digital environment people can make themselves more beautiful than they ever could by wearing makeup. If you happen to be Maybelline or Vogue, you might say, who cares? We still make money.

Well, to a point. Many fashion brands are scaling back. Instead of saying we are still making money, another view is: why did we let a new audience get away from us? Why did we not serve the digital native?

Enter Meitu. The Chinese beauty app Meitu allows people to make themselves look better online. It enables digital beauty. The company launched an initial public offering (IPO) in December 2016 valuing it at $4 billion. Raising $630 million, it then moved its product base into video. At the time of writing Meitu apps (beauty and video) have been installed 1 billion times and the company receives 8 billion views a month for the video site where it has recruited snappy, self-made Gen Z celebs to speak directly to its audiences.

Meitu disintermediates existing advertising platforms and it speaks directly to its users. It can also dictate terms to fashion brands. It has direct daily contact with people who are the future customers of high fashion in the fastest growing markets in the world and are beautifying their lives now.

Meitu began life in 2008 but most of its success has come in the past five years. By having a direct, digital relationship with customers, it can know anything and everything about their beauty needs (the lipstick shades they choose, hair type, the vloggers they like to follow and so on). It has the opportunity to foster a natural segmentation based on users' tastes (a bit like Netflix has in movies and TV programming). This is considerably more powerful than the old fashion value chain (suppliers, designers, manufacturers, fashion retailers, print magazines), easier to manage and much less costly.

Old fashion brands missed out on digital beauty. They suffered not just because they did not see these new apps arriving. They missed out because they relied on their existing personas. They had a fixed view of how their customers respond to trends. They failed to dive into emerging customer segments.

Meitu's genius lies in its ability to respond to a vibrant audience. Clearly the company has technical assets but it also has agility and an ability to spot and promote stars. Its assets have been technical (also in image processing and pattern recognition, Cloud skills, app development, scaling) but also talent spotting and promotion. The compact with its new stars is every bit as powerful as Airbnb's compact with property owners. Speed has been another asset.

Meitu now has what YouTube, Apple and any large platform has. An ecosystem of partners that feeds the long-tail needs of its users. When you have these types of segmentations then innovation is defined by the relationships the audience has with the platform's partners. Both Meitu and its celebrities can offer new products to the market and get immediate reactions, often before anything is sold. The types of products it offers, largely to the 16-23 years age bracket are: face slimming software, skin buffing, lengthening limbs and applying makeup; filters, frames and effects; teeth whitening, auto-tweaks; ecommerce shopping; video apps; video content; video re-touch; gifting; advertising; Meitu smartphones specified for selfie experiences, stabilisation, low light shooting, and limited edition smartphones. It's hunger to create new products is alarming!

Initially a stand alone app, the brand is now an umbrella for celebrities in just the way YouTube is. It also has partnerships with mainstream sites like WeChat, Baidu and Google.

A fashion company might have spotted people's desire for digital beautification before Meitu were it better positioned to assess up-stream value changes. But we now live in an economy where it is possible for startups, or any other competitor, to spot or create an unmet need or poorly served customers, move in with a new offer based around a platform and a low-cost of customer acquisition, seize the upstream opportunity and pick up all the downstream value.

EXAMPLE 2: FINANCE

Here's a further example from the finance industry. Currency conversion and remittance companies, like TransferWise and CurrencyFair, as well as many companies in working capital provi-sion, spotted that banks have very weak customer segmentation. We will look at this area by applying the model we introduced earlier: customer segmentation; asset discovery; targeted ideation; and eco-system building. We had that in mind above when we discussed Meitu but now we want to be more explicit.

Customer segmentation: Many retail banks think of their seg-mentation as: *account holders*, *premium account holders* and *high net* *worth individuals.* 3 segments with various sized business accounts rounding out the retail portfolio.

Over the past decade, though, smaller companies have grown their "exotic currency" needs as they traded into non-core areas (markets outside the Euro, dollar and sterling zones). These smaller companies had wandered into the area of global trade, enabled by the Web. It meant currency exchange and international payments suddenly became major cost issues for them. This is very much the upstream insights' challenge for any incumbent. It is not easy to spot the trend (though not impossible either) or to convince colleagues that upstream changes in segment demand like this warrant changes in the business operating model.

The banks were not simply being ignorant of their customers' changing circumstances, however. They were blindsided by a lack of attention to a specific insights problem (the upstream challenge).

There was, at the same time, a growing migrant population that needed to send money back to their home communities. As with the small companies' segment, the banks' reaction was to stick with their existing operational model and do nothing.

Asset discovery: New currency services spotted these trends. They have tried to serve different segments (personal and small business) and TransferWise in particular has been highly experimental in trying to reach its audiences.

The problem for these companies is that they have stuck to far too narrow a range of services. The story they tell of undercutting banks is popular enough that it can even be used to disguise their own high fees. Most of their segmentation has been on the sales side, figuring out ways to uncover buyer segments. Segmentation tends to be country-specific and corridor specific (transferring money from the UK to Bangladesh, for example). But their product range is actually very narrow. In effect they are bank-to-bank transfer services without much else in the till.

Arguably they have not gone far enough with their customer segmentation and operational models. But let's not be over critical. It is difficult for a startup to think about asset discovery because essentially they are involved in platform building. Their assets are their skills and market knowledge. Within those constraints new currency services have done well. But they have not scaled in the way that business platforms often do. They have not become exponential. They need to think more about new services for many new segments.

Targeted ideation: That's not to say, however, that they have lacked segmentation and targeted innovation completely. Currencyfair was initially set up by entrepreneurs from Ireland, Australia and the UK who spotted a strong source of demand from those three markets. They built a global service from those origins and they introduced a marketplace early on for customers who fancied themselves as speculators. However, their lack of secondary products and tools suggests the lack of true customer segmentation leaves them bereft of good ideas for new tools or services.

Ecosystem: This currency marketplace has allowed Currencyfair to develop an ecosystem of customers who are part speculators and part savers. Their marketplace is underdeveloped. Many marketplaces and platforms stay that way. But they could expand. They could use the cash in the marketplace, and the trust they have generated, to fund small working capital loans. They also have an ecosystem of banking partners and payment rails they work with and could draw them into a broader array of services.

Still, pure currency conversion and transfer startups have left a lot on the table. As the smaller businesses we referred to above were growing they encountered a need for working capital. They were encountering longer payment periods too, adding to that need.

Google, Alibaba, and Amazon, know that banks do poor working-capital provision to small businesses. These tech platforms have now moved into this market. They will come to dominate it because they have data on a small firm's trading and receivables that can reduce the cost of risky lending. They can also automate the decision process to a large extent, saving even more cost.

In Alibaba's case, they can also help promote companies who are going through a sticky patch. By the way, which company poses a threat to the market for home improvement lending? Yes, Airbnb.

In summary, poor customer segmentation has presented multiple threats to banks and allowed new market dynamics to grow.

THE IMPORTANCE OF DYNAMIC CUSTOMER SEGMENTATION

Today's markets are characterised by a totally different set of *economies of scope* that change the nature of market segmentation and upstream value.

To understand the challenge presented by economies of scope, think about conventional management theory. For decades executives have been told to stick to a core competency and avoid adjacencies.

An adjacency would be, say, a concrete manufacturer being naturally close to the housing market, and its ebbs and flows, deciding to selling lawn mowers. Great idea but it nearly sunk Blue Circle, a major European concrete-maker whose adjacencies were ill-judged. So too, Kodak which moved in to a field of chemicals' manufacture that lay outside its knowledge base. In the days of limited computing power and poor market information, businesses were wary of adjacent businesses for a good reason.

In those darn old conservative days, businesses had a narrow idea of what an economy of scope could mean (explained below). Today major platforms use economies of scope as a natural part of dominating broad-based markets. They sell millions of different products!!!

An economy of scope in the past was not so challenging. It could be, OK I sell toothpaste, would I not try selling toothbrushes too and floss? These are near-adjacencies with identical distribution channels. But even those tightly knit adjacencies used to be thought of as racy. Toothpaste is what you know!

Since 2007 and the rise of Amazon and Alibaba, and platform businesses in general, we now know that companies can handle millions of different products and still stay focused on customer success. Inventory is important. In other words economies of scope have come of age.

Because of that, knowing your customer segmentation is more important than ever. Economies of scope function through long-tail markets. That term is somewhat forgotten these days. It simply means that markets are highly segmented not by you but by customers. They make surprising associations between different types of products. That is to say, we are not aiming to sell a toothbrush to someone who buys our toothpaste. We now aim to sell relatively obscure Tibetan salt to the same person who opts for a New Zealand shower gel and Aloe Vera toothpaste. And what's more they might enjoy Beatles' memorabilia and Agatha Christie novels. That's what the long-tail is all about. People have complex tastes and it is the genius of companies like Amazon to find ways to tap into all their natural segments.

The challenges of segmentation and customer success are also complicated by the arrival of microtrends. Mastercard now look to these microtrends - something that might evolve in the market and die over a three day period - to create a micro-market or micro-advantage. Companies want micro-segments and micro-trends. And they need to deliver something of value to these fruit-fly markets ultra-fast. To be really customer-centric, therefore, is to realise that innovation is no longer about creating a new product. It is about creating a new approach to customers.

DEVELOPING A CUSTOMER INNOVATION WALL AS A STARTPOINT FOR AGILE BUSINESS

Keeping segmentation under review is essential in a long-tail economy. In Flow, we use deeper customer segmentations to make innovation more targeted. Deeper segmentations help spot unmet needs and they help align assets with those needs.

With Flow we are looking at how we can create the right conversations around this. Using a Customer Innovation Wall, for example, opens up a dialogue about the types of customers you have, the qualities that are changing in the customer base, the innovations that are likely to contribute to customer success, and the types of assets you now need to get hold of or develop. Dynamic segmentation provides a lot of advantages.

- It helps you target innovation at specific groups and specific needs, ensuring you meet hidden needs.

- It alerts you to the range of potential micro-markets and micro-trends.

- It is a buffer against disruption.

- It allows you to think of specific customer success factors in long-tail niches. By that we mean you can think how you can make more customers successful in what they do.

- It allows you to develop economies of scope, i.e. by offering multiple products into many niches - and we are in the age of scale, scope and speed.

The Customer Innovation Wall is a venue to discuss segmentation, assets and ecosystems. There are some complicated ideas there so we won't try to explain them all in one go (please see Chapter 12 for more). Here is a Customer Innovation Wall.

A SAMPLE CUSTOMER INNOVATION WALL

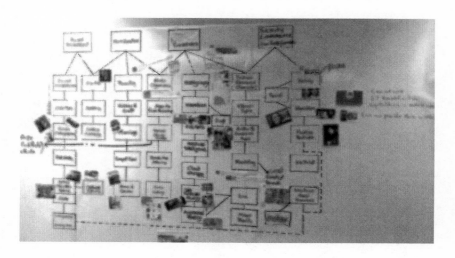

We have blurred the detail out of this image for reasons of confidentiality. It comes from a company that previously divided its customer base into one or two main segments. You can see that we now have multiple new segments. We later draw on actual quotes from people within those segments (plenty of people blog and tweet so we went in search of what they were saying). We also included photographs of people whose comments are insightful.

We leave the Wall to develop as people pass by. Anybody can add a segment or make a comment about a segment or propose a new idea for adding value to that segment. In this way customer segmentation can be a conversational part of company culture.

How do you go about creating something like this? First you have to believe it is useful to build part of your workspace out of your customers' activities. Second, you already have access to a huge amount of information that customers volunteer through their social media activity and when they call you. If your products are digital you have usage patterns. You don't have to buy up information collected in dubious ways.

We use social media tools to help identify the range of interests of a company's keenest fans. We rely on Michael Hussey's StatSocial for this but you could also use Sprinklr, Crimson Hexagon and any number of others that might give you a structured overview of customer interests.

What do these analytical tools show? Here's an example. We already said that people who follow mass market cars tend also to follow websites and blogs that reference bicycles. There is a segment of the car buying public that loves cycling. That is good information. Are you providing enough in your showrooms or distributorships for people who probably use their cars to transport their bikes? Why are you not in the cycle business?

Social media data can tell you a lot about your segments. However, the segmentation does not come ready made. You have to think about it. It should be the focal point of conversations. First you want to be figuring out new segments, then identify what unmet needs might exist, and then what assets you have or can gain access to, to serve those needs.

The point we emphasise is that this knowledge of segments is what gives a startup an advantage. They look for unmet needs. You have to explore those too. But it cannot be a one-off exercise. It has to be part of daily practice.

RE-ORGANISING INNOVATION FOR AGILITY

In the rest of this chapter we are going to show you how to build up a Customer Innovation Wall. We will discuss how segmentation can become part of routine conversations with segments on the Wall ready to be developed further. In a typical segment you will find unmet needs. From that insight you can develop new ideas. This new ideas can find their way into the Flow to be tested. But very often you will already have assets that can meet those needs. Innovation can be met by redeploying existing assets. Or it could be you will choose to develop an ecosystem of partners who have assets that are better placed to serve your customers. The tasks we are going to discuss are the CATE ones we introduced earlier:

CUSTOMER SEGMENTATION, ASSET DISCOVERY, TARGETED IDEATION, AND ECOSYSTEM BUILDING.

Each is important to business agility. To grasp their importance, we need to start by rethinking assets.

In highly innovative organisations, people are capable of switching their view of what constitutes assets and how to harness them. Assets are tangible and intangible but they also might not belong to you. Great companies exploit third party assets. This is actually not such a new idea. Banks have always done it. But applied more pervasively (rooms, cars, tools, aircraft, experiences) it has created a new kind of economy.

Good segmentation allows you to get a better view of assets and where they can be used. Remember the sequence:

1.   The first is the customer segmentation.

2.   The second is the exploration of the company's existing assets (known and hidden).

3.   The third is the exploration of new ways to bring success to these segments.

4.   The fourth is to focus on the ecosystem partners that can make this easier or scaleable.

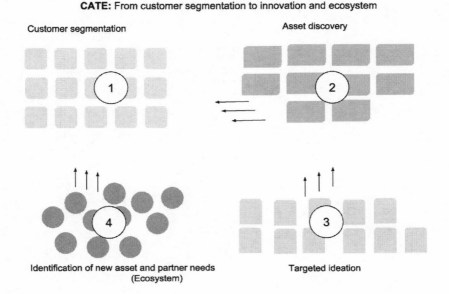

CATE: From customer segmentation to innovation and ecosystem

Customer segmentation

Asset discovery

Identification of new asset and partner needs
(Ecosystem)

Targeted ideation

EXAMPLE 1: GOING FROM SEGMENTATION TO NEW ASSETS AND PRODUCTS

Let's look at an example. In Africa many NGOs task themselves with improving financial inclusion *for the poor.*

"The poor" is some kind of market segment. It can be defined by disposable income but actually that is not the be all and end all of it. In Kenya, for example, there are tribes that oblige members to distribute surplus resources to other tribe members. A couple with two cows have wealth but they have to give much of the milk they produce to neighbours. They are actually quite poor, even in their own terms.

"The poor" often only makes sense in terms of western income values. It is a line ($20 per month) below which people are said to lack…. something essential.

A brief reflection on this though and you can break down this idea of "the poor" into many segments, some of which have no immediate use for financial services as defined by banks.

Customer segmentation: People who work in financial inclusion do a tremendous job but when segmenting this market it becomes clear there are people with resources who do not want regular financial services. When we started to think this way we were able to create a much wider segmentation of the poor as a market. Some of that is reproduced below. It is the beginning of a Customer Innovation Wall for the financially excluded.

Beginning a Customer Innovation Wall of the financially excluded or "poor"

Unbanked but resourced	Wealthy but poor	Hustlers	Low paid
Pastoralists	Subsistence farmers	Catering gangs	Flower workers
Mutatu drivers	Small-scale livestock owners	Water sellers	Labourers
Bike taxis	Fruit and flower growers	Illicit bar owners	Herdsmen
Chamas			Catering trades

Let's review some of these groups. Pastoralists on the Tanzanian border give their market-day money to local shops who then use it as working-capital while the pastoralist goes back to the hills.

Technically, the pastoralist can be poor. He might not meet a certain income threshold. In reality, he creates the financial services he needs within this community. For him, cash is a handicap most of the time. He is about to go off walking in the hills for a month where cash has no value. However, it does have value to the local ironmonger or clothes shop so that's where he leaves it. The ironmonger, dress shop and other retailers get cash to buy supplies. And they do not need to go to a bank for that. By the time the pastoralist walks back into town, these shopkeepers have bought and sold their goods. They are ready to return his money.

Mutatus are self-employed drivers who own their own buses. They transport people as well as goods. Smaller towns in Africa will also have people providing taxi services on the back of cheap Chinese motorbikes. These people have assets but they function in cash wherever possible.

Other people, often referred to as hustlers, only get work because they are prepared (and happy) to accept payment in cash. Hustlers might be selling fruit by the roadside or bottles of water to overheated drivers on a very hot day. Gangmasters want 20 waiters for a middle class wedding, but only for that one event. People in the slums operate bars and other businesses, creating a financially well-functioning ghetto rather than a well of poverty.

All these people are excluded from financial services as defined by the banking system. But they are a diverse group all with different financial needs.

Workers in the flower industry, on the other hand, one of Kenya's largest industries, can be paid through a bank or via the mobile money service, M-Pesa. However, they do not earn a living wage. Many of the other people in full-time work rely on mobile credit from M-Pesa's owner Safaricom, credit they are unlikely to repay. They have access to financial services, in other words, but are both poor and indebted.

The real segmentation in this financial market is extremely diverse. The potential customers of aid and banks need a variety of services. They, themselves, create diverse services to meet their needs (the Chamas, for example. are self-organised credit groups).

The finance industry, however, has not explored the patterns of emerging customer financial needs and instead lumps them all under "poor." Policy makers in the donor community do the same. Using the terms "poor" or "financially excluded" actually masks a lot of opportunity for different types of services or no service. That is the reason why we suggest detailed and continuous customer segmentations. We need to be constantly seeking areas to add value.

Asset discovery: The asset base of each of these groups is different. On the left there is a variety of assets like goats, buses and bike-taxis that are used to earn cash. In the next column people have land but have no working capital. They often struggle to access markets because they cannot quality mark their food and they have no scale or transportation.

The left hand column appears to be in fairly good stead. The people with land are the ones who are stuck. They have assets such as mobile phones/global connectivity and relatively good coverage. In fact, the second of these is an overlooked asset. These communities are globally connected. Most have mobile phones and many have feature phones. To date there has been little attempt to leverage this *global* network.

They also have a variety of social mores that mean they are unlikely to be abandoned by their community or tribe. But their problems are multi-generational as they often cannot afford to educate their children fully.

Targeted ideation: There is very little point in innovating for the poor or having a general policy of financial inclusion. Financial services are often self-provided or community based. But by looking at the assets available and unmet needs, it might be possible to get creative and provide some new services. Let's apply that thinking to the small landowner with livestock.

The obvious missing assets for this segment are cash flow, market access, transportation and scale. But there is a hidden asset. Africa will be the target of multiple eco-finance transfers in the next decade.

Having land means smallholders should be able to participate in global carbon sequestration projects or funding for alternative land-use.

They also have the luxury of fertile land in an arid country. They simply have no way to exploit these assets to anything like the degree possible. They need new forms of revenue and perhaps also better connectivity and communications. They also lack some essentials for good land-use: knowledge, irrigation and power.

Asset identification and ideation

Segment	Assets	Hidden Assets	Missing assets/ Unmet needs	Ideas
Small-scale, settled livestock owners	Land Connectivity Animals	Social support Carbon sequestration? Global connectivity	Cash flow Market access Scale Irrigation Electricity	

In becoming customer-centric it is very useful to create visual Walls to map these things out. In Flow, we want everything to be visual so we set out an account of assets and the ideas they help us generate.

The review of assets and unmet needs suggests a few new options.

- Generate working capital by crowdfunding the expansion of smallholdings using a dedicated global crowdfunding site.

- Replace local micro-loans (interest rate 40%) with global micro-investments (using digital platforms to reduce cost and build data), encouraging the farming community globally to invest in expansion in Africa.

- Have donors create a new class of credit for adaptation to global warming (such as mini-sequestration projects) to generate guaranteed income.

- Support carbon sequestration techniques (also to generate guaranteed revenue).

- Have global retailers sponsor local transportation networks (the Uber of local markets).

The innovations can be very varied once you identify segments and explore assets. A thorough analysis would suggest many more. That's the Flow credo. These Walls are never done. They are never finished. The Wall below is an account of initial ideas for small farm innovation and revenues.

Ideation

	Crowdfund	P2P micro-loan platform	Carbon sequestration	GHG adaptation	Sponsorship
Evaluate task size and prioritise	$	$	$$$	$$$	

■ Large work area   ▢ Small work area

$, $$, $$$

The ecosystem: The Post-Its represent the presumed scale of each initiative and there are some dollar signs attached too. But this is phase 1 of a process that will see work broken down further while more accurate evaluations take place. Of course when you start to break this work down, you want to be specific about the goals of each work area and each work unit. However, at this stage you are going to be very broad brush.

Looking at this, it appears as though you can get a quick win, a short route to value, by opening discussions with existing crowdfunding and P2P platforms. And you can see, it is the really novel options that will be tough going. They should not be ducked but a value-seeking approach would jump on the quick wins while work on the longer term is being assessed. However, finding partners that can become a broader ecosystem is a good strategy. Over time you can deepen your knowledge of what that ecosystem might be and how to nurture it. Here, we are in the early stages.

There are two things of note now. You are going to break all this work down and it might be that quick routes to value also lie in the tougher work areas. You will only know by looking. Resist the temptation to say of any one action: It will never work. Second you are beginning to see the need for the ecosystem, partners who will help your innovation become a reality. To get to that, you will need to start thinking about a content strategy, a topic we will return to in Chapter 12.

One final point. In this process you will begin to refresh your goals for your mission or project.

Setting goals: The ideation above needs to be turned into a Portfolio Wall where we start to make estimates of value, timing, and priority. But before we do that we have to ask questions about our goals.

Traditionally the goal in aid programs has been to alleviate poverty through financial inclusion. Arguing against this would be counterproductive. Financial inclusion, though, has been taken to mean the use of banks. Yet it is clear from this list that mechanisms such as crowdfunding, global P2P micro-loans, carbon credits or adaptation credits and so on can be useful financial measures.

The goal should actually be to facilitate growth and stability and the ideas we have come up with need to be judged against that. That goal can go on as the lead objective for an Executive Portfolio Wall (Chapter 7).

EXAMPLE 2: TUNING UP THE CAR INDUSTRY

In the auto industry, segmentation is usually done by income group or model line-up - saloon cars for executives, SUVs for families, starter cars for young drivers; sportier cars for petrolheads.

The interesting element of the western car industry is that mass market manufacturers make their money on parts rather than on the car itself. They are in the Wilkinson Sword business model.

Executives forget this. They have bought into the idea that their future lies in big data and the market of one - the single view of the customer. Most auto-companies have launched massive data projects that will take years to come to some kind of fruition. Will they ever yield the customer preferences data that consistently allows car makers to offer the right product with the right terms and conditions to make the right kind of sale?

Possibly, but it is a long way off. When all cars are autonomous and are funnelling new kinds of data to the car maker then the perfect sell will enter the cross-hairs.

Meantime, big companies admire big systems and car makers are sold on the idea that they can access data that has the same power as that enjoyed by companies such as Netflix. There's a clue of course as to why Netflix will make better use of big data.

Netflix has to continuously monitor and assess what type of content interests people. They can do this by interaction and observing consumption patterns across an audience of 100 million people. But a car-is-a-car-is-a-car. There's not a fantastic amount to learn about what people think of them or to adapt how the car performs, yet.

The single view of the customer mantra also overlooks the fact that in the Wilkinson Sword model, at least for large purchases, the decisive factor is getting people to return regularly for a dose of the Kool Aid - in the case of cars that means servicing.

It is very difficult to see what big data will give a company in the way of relationship building insights to stop customers drifting off to much cheaper servicing alternatives at the local mechanic's garage. It is clear, however, that a better segmentation of the customer base could give us plenty of ways to make servicing a better experience. In this case, of course, we are dealing with a different perspective on upstream value. Here, the car has been sold so we need value markers that help us continuously build a relationship.

GETTING INTO THE FLOW WITH CUSTOMER SOCIAL DATA

In Flow we are committed to small steps rather than big, big projects. The returning customer problem has a solution. Understanding customers by talking with them. A quick way into their views is available through social data.

Analysing the interests of mass market car owners through social media data, they appear to be more diverse than product line-ups suggest. In fact, reviewing the interests of mass market car owners you see things like:

1. Big switching potential as many also follow luxury brands BMW and Mercedes.

2. A disproportionate interest in "upmarket" sports such as cricket and rugby (especially among those following After-Sales) compared to fans of global sport brands such as Cristiano Ronaldo in the car sales segment.

3. A love of poetry (Paulo Coelho features large).

4. Heroes such as Jeremy Clarkson and Bill Gates, as well as a love of business and especially real estate.

5. Languages.

6. Cycling.

7.   Motorbikes.

8.   Vintage cars.

9.   Wine.

10. Only 25% of followers of mainstream car makers are female even though they make up over 50% of car buyers and 80% of purchase decision makers.

11. Over 35% of people following After-Sales are women.

12. Millennials, while under-represented (as are ethnic groups) in cars, are the largest group in After-Sales.

13. Overall car enthusiasts have a disproportionate interest in e-commerce compared to the population at large but are less likely to follow money-saving sites.

14. Have a very high level of interest in rentals. Interestingly, we found little evidence of an interest in car-sharing.

15. Are generally travel enthusiasts.

16. In parts and services, customers are more disposed towards international news and travel than those who follow car models, maybe indicating a group that looks beyond their immediate circumstances.

17. Are more likely to be interested in radio than the average online social media user.

18. Are more prone to gamification.

19. Are more likely than the average person to be interested in sports' participation such as jogging or mountain biking.

This type of data took about two hours to collate. Normally a customer survey would take place over months. But Flow is focused on what we can learn now rather than the alternative of putting value deep into the future.

Customer segmentation: Social data can help develop a new segmentation that will already start triggering ideas for innovation. What's more, the innovation that follows will be targeted.

Beginning a Customer Innovation Wall in Autos

Switchers	Lifestyle Drivers	Car geeks	After sales
BMW/Merc fans	Worldly / issue-driven	Sport car fans	Women
Cycling geeks	Travel enthusiasts	Vintage	Switchers
Leadership aspirationalists	Cultural reachers	Upmarket	Millennials
Eco-warriors	Online / ecommerce jockeys	Rally enthusiasts	Gen Z
	Radio listeners	Moto GP	Renters
	Sports fans	Logistics professionals	Gamers
	Mindfulness people		

The segmentation above is a beginning for a Customer Innovation Wall. It is paint on the wall for people to critique and shape.

Asset discovery: So what are the obvious, hidden and unknown assets in After-Sales? An obvious asset of distributorships is real estate. Often they have plenty of showroom space. Another asset is that people have to visit each day. There is a guaranteed footfall though it is small. Distributors have strong mailing lists and they have the potential for nationally branded advertising. Their employees are generally skilled at fixing electronic and mechanical parts.

The car manufacturer will have all types of software much of which now interacts with customers (OnStar, navigation systems, websites). There are also plenty of mobility apps out there. The search for assets should go on and on.

Asset identification and ideation

Segment	Assets	Hidden Assets	Missing assets/ Unmet needs	Ideas
Female After-Sales	Retail space Customer information Car performance data Mechanical and electronic skills	Global brand	Sexual neutrality Cost transparency Local transport Trust Poor digital know-how	

Targeted ideation: The missing assets are things like a dearth of digital know-how and a lack of expertise in digital marketing. There is often an extreme gender imbalance (women make up only 16% of the repair workforce in Europe and 8% in the US), which is clearly a liability.

Other groups that could be targeted are the millennial fans of After-Sales sites; those with a strong interest in travel; people stretching themselves culturally; people who appear to be actively looking to switch; those with a strong interest in sport and sports' participation, especially mountain biking, and other mobility interests, whether that be cycling or vintage cars and memorabilia, and people who want to shop online.

There are also unmet needs and therefore many missing assets that third parties might be able to help with. People find it difficult to get to garages when they also have the school run to do.

It can be difficult for them to get into work from garages. Nobody seems to have looked at the "customer journey" beyond taking the car off them.

There is sometimes a suspicion of the garage's inability or unwillingness to be totally transparent about the car's repair needs. There is a hidden unmet need too. Manufacturers are global, whereas distributors are local. One is a supply-chain-oriented company; the other is retail. There is not much in between to create new ideas that have local applicability across a wide area (State, region etc.).

That might explain why car companies are interested in big data (they are large companies) and miss out on proper customer segmentation (it is in the hands of the distributor). We think that a good antidote to big projects is to ask what can be done to improve customer satisfaction next week or the week after? Flow activity thrives on the next action.

There is no need for a big data project to answer questions like: Are women adequately catered for in distributor garages, especially those on the edge of town? A small research project would help you find out. We mentioned earlier our observation that women can feel aggressed in garages, fear the process lacks transparency, find it difficult to juggle the garage visit with other responsibilities, are put on the defensive, and feel mis-sold to.

Long before a big data project got under way, auto-makers could be improving the experience for a disproportionately important segment in the After-Sales market. They have to ask what they can do to help bring more success to female After-Sales' customers. Over time they can break this "segment" down into smaller segments where they can find even more value but for now let's stay high level.

Equally, without spending a fortune, a company can start to figure out how to serve drivers who also love bikes. Creating a bike rental station outside the dealership would help contribute to multiple success factors.

The ecosystem: Three examples will help illustrate how these kinds of data (and there is much more of it) can help build innovation strategies.

1. After-Sales, where your profits are, is a primary concern of female drivers. But how many distributors prioritise female customers at garages? There is a host of ways to do that to improve loyalty and to build margins for exceptional service by asking about customer success. We went into this in detail in *Flow.…* But ideas like partnering with third party transport providers is one; having a stronger female workforce quickly trained up would be another. Car companies need to ask what assets and partners they can quickly bring into play on these solutions.

2. Cycling. What's the fastest growing form or urban transport globally? Bikes. And many of the customers of car salesrooms actually want also to ride bikes, so what could you do with all that distribution real-estate or with your business model to serve these customers better? What is your mobility ecosystem?

3. Design for gamification. The final point is that we should take gamification into account in any digital design. It is difficult for us to envision what that might be. We are not game designers. But many garages are monuments to old industry, with all its bad habits. They need to become digital and diverse.

Looked at this way, we are trying to move:

From: How can I cross-sell and up-sell or entice customers back?

To: How can I create success for my customers? How can I help them achieve goals that they set for themselves and of course profit by providing them with that value?

Better is not more up-sell - up-selling cars is great for distributors but it can poison a car-makers' credit portfolio and reputation. Up-selling can be disastrous. Instead we need to align with customer success. It is worth reading the work of people like Lincoln Murphy in the SaaS environment on this important topic.

These are just small examples of customer segmentation insights. in Flow we seek out customer value all the time. When we break work down (Chapters 5 and 6) and when we prioritise time-use, value for customers drives all decisions. But we also said an important point for the next stage of work is to set new goals.

Stating goals: Companies in situations like this need to state goals in terms of customer success. The idea of having a better view of the customer through data is fine as far as it goes. But the result will be more selling. What is actually needed is a goal that increases customer success. Something like, I want female customers to be shown due respect, to create provision for safe onward mobility, or to have women leave and return happy. These are real goals.

Customer Insight Walls and Customer Innovation Walls can force the issue of customer success to become a daily concern - as it should be. They help shape people's thinking around value. We'll go into this idea further in Step 6 where we will more closely relate segmentation to value and to work breakdown. More later.

Every company will find that their fan-base wants something more from them. The journey from segmentation to innovation and ecosystem can prime you to deliver to those needs. Good customer segmentation can help start the flow of innovation. But to respond to more segments, companies need to be able to deliver a broader array of services and features. To do that they need to disrupt the cadence of work.

CHAPTER 3

Disrupting The Cadence of Work

An agile business does more work, more quickly and pivots when it needs to, before wasting resources. To be that business you need new ways to work. But here's a situation you might find familiar. You've been in a wildly productive team meeting. You've done something amazing like designing the units of work needed for a killer app. It is a breakthrough moment. The design work was informed by a much better customer segmentation so you are sure you are hitting the right mark. The work took only a couple of hours but it is bang on. Great collaboration. You all want to get started, then a team leader says: Okay, I'll write that one up. If your workplace bears any resemblance to the many we've seen, that task of "writing the project up" will land with a thud.

The normal expectation of "writing it up" is about a three week turnaround. That's not because the writing-up job will take three weeks. It could take a day or less. But the cadence of work in your organisation allows three weeks. It's part of the culture. What's also likely, by the way, is that the write up will not match what you took from that meeting, in the moment. The consensus will inevitably be broken by time and the perspective of that guy writing it up.

As you look around at the Wall where you've all been busy ideating, the experience of being inspired by colleagues resonates one more time. You are raring to go. So, you wonder, what really needs writing up? Everything you need to get going is there on Post-It notes, neatly arranged, logically structured, incorporating IT, logistics and marketing. It needs another round of work to get it on to the Kanban Wall for task allocation. But it doesn't need "writing up".

Because of the cadence of work, action is at least three weeks away, and probably more given the same cadence of work creates more delays as you seek agreement on resources.

This just takes the wind out of your sails. You know this great project is actually going to die. The "write it up guy" will have other work to do and three weeks will become Neverland. By the time you get this group together again, it will be for the next promising idea.

The reality is most work does not need a project plan nor a GANTT chart and nor really does it need a budget. What it needs is somebody to take control of the cadence of work. Flow is a movement for faster work that stays social and accountable:

1. Use a photograph of the afternoon's session, in place of a write up; a photo or two of the people involved to post on an Appreciation Wall (because you did great work together).

2. Create tweet length high level value statements about the work, why it will be good for customers and how you can get that tested with them, ASAP.

3. Invest in further work breakdown to identify tasks that need doing first (which should be posted on the Team Kanban Wall) and a commitment to do a new set of work breakdowns once the first set is in development (set the date).

4. Do a rough estimate of resources based on the number of units of work at 2 day cycle-time.

5. Have a conversation with a test designer/ QA to figure out what would be "acceptable" in terms of the first iteration of delivery.

6. Transfer the overall set of units to a Project Wall.

Taking all of activity needed to produce these steps, you should really be able to do it in another 2 x 2 hour sessions. Movements don't hang around. This work could be done the same day or the next day. More likely the work will go to a backlog and take its turn, but we're pretty sure you get the point. There's no reason to wait three weeks to summarise good work into a plan or longer to find a good project dead. The three week wait turns into an eternity. Great projects get lost this way.

In the modern workplace you are going to rely on customer feedback for your decisions about value. You and I don't need to make those judgments or to pretend we can second guess them. We will make a few informal guesstimates, but our job is to get ideas in front of customers, quickly. To do that we involve a lot of people in just-in-time decisions about what customers might be interested in, what they should be shown first, and what tests will trigger any further work on an initiative.

These just-in-time principles, discussions, arguments and tests replace the plan. We create value when we see it, not because we have a plan where we have speculated on where the value might be, how long it will take to realise and how much it will cost. Value comes out of discussions and interactions at the right venues (Walls).

To get to this new place, the cadence of work has to be disrupted. That guy who wants to "write it up" needs to be stopped. Ban reports. Put a stop to plans. Take photographs instead. Photos trump all kinds of text. Trust the image. Otherwise you will be waiting months before a customer gets to see a feature that you think has value. By then it could be too late because the market opportunity will be on the wane.

If you can disrupt the cadence of work, if you can tear up your assumptions about how long things take and agree on a maximum two-day cycle-time (more below), you will be able to deliver any number of new ideas from your Customer Innovation Wall.

CREATING CONTINUOUS INNOVATION

Flow philosophy makes work more social, more interactive, less structured, more visual and less command-driven. And that idea of co-designing is really important. Work isn't meant to go into somebody's desk drawer or to be hidden away on a laptop. It is meant to sit on the Walls of the building where it can be shared. In this chapter we will also underline the point that work is value driven and value often starts by stating flexible goals that represent a growing sense of what you believe has value. Those goals are the link between the CATE model we introduced in the last chapter and the new cadence of work.

This new way of working originated in Kanban, in manufacturing. It was taken up in software but it is applicable throughout the firm if people are willing to take the simple steps we outline in this book.

The basic principles remain constant wherever they are applied. Flow is about social interaction and visualisation and not about hierarchy, reports and plans. It is about planning in real time and rejecting the mythical cadences that allow people to fulfill their roles rather than creating something new or additional. It's about calling out the time we all waste.

The decision to go to a new cadence sparks a revolution in work practices. All work needs breaking down so that the maximum time away from the Wall is 2 days.

For business agility to take hold, however, an important prerequisite is for people outside of the IT department to gain some understanding of what is changing in IT practices. Modern IT is undergoing a revolution (though some CIOs manage to hide that fact or shy away from it). These changes will help you to deliver more innovation and more value much more often. It can also liberate people to work with a renewed sense of purpose.

Having systems that allow people to change their minds and shift direction (or pivot) quickly - well, that is a vital competitive resource, like blood is to the body. But critically, humans interact around a purpose and modern IT is flexible enough for purpose to re-enter work life. We can banish old systems and controls.

But you have to change the idea that work takes a certain amount of time simply because that's the way it always got done. You transform an organisation by shaking off those attitudes and assumptions. Reduced cycle-time is key to the liberation.

Reduced cycle-time enables continuous innovation. It lets you break out of outdated work cadences. And it takes you away from rules towards emotions and relationships. Reduced cycle-time gives us:

- Purpose - the shared sense that we are seeking value together.

- The capacity to discriminate value from waste and to deliver value continuously.

- The capacity to innovate every day.

- A culture of flexible goals rather than plans (a point we emphasised in Chapter 2).

Here's how to start the journey.

(FLEXIBLE) GOAL-DRIVEN WORK DESIGN

Building on what we said in Chapter 2, we now want to use the example of creating an online survey of people who follow car brands. This kind of task is interesting because it demonstrates that there can be no IT-Business divide when companies function properly.

The type of work involves IT and the business together. Traditionally it would have been stated as a requirement by the business and handed over to the former for translating into an IT project with deliverables, milestones, sprints and a delivery date.

The digital nature of work, however, means we can recompose that idea into something more shared, more dynamic, and not only shorter but also highly visible, interactive and driven by goals. Goals are outcomes that we could assign a value to.

Here is a very simple example and an illustration of the principles. All of this takes place at a Project Wall. The ambition is to take no more than two days to design the survey, two days to get it online, two days to execute, and a day to analyse and interpret. In what follows we are driven by those time-scales.

Here's how the work might initially breakdown, listing task areas by their owner.

GOALS

Task / Assigned to	Organise consensus on goals	Anticipate outcomes	Automate process and analysis	Ensure quality
Flow value manager	Analyse requirements Organise standup	Draft and categorise key questions Express potential contribution to goals	Support developer	Pilot the survey
Business analyst		Support Flow owner	Select tools	Create reporting template
Developer			Design gamified survey Design landing page	Consult UX designer / test with colleagues
Social media expert		Research examples of prior art		Create online content so customers discover the survey, and optimise

Tasks

How would you get to this kind of matrix, bearing in mind it is only a preliminary, before tasks are further broken down?

The reality is that different teams will identify different goals and go about it in different ways. The significant role of a leader in this situation is to let a conversation develop and to keep driving the conversation back to goals. The other important role is to provide support to people who are looking, initially, at a blank wall. The creative process has to be iterative, going from a blank wall to a few ideas to something more structured. But people need to be given confidence that they will not be judged on any intermediate stage. And they need emotional resilience, because they are going to face critique.

HERE IS HOW WE ARRIVED AT THOSE GOALS:

Filling the blank sheet of paper

Logic   Draft goal

What do we really want out of the survey? We want to avoid the temptation to organise it so people just say nice things about us. This is about them, the customer and their success. We need agreement on this at each stage of the project.   1

If we are going to do it quickly we can't ask too many questions (initial limit 10 and let's see how that works) and we need to know that each question relates to some potential information about improving their success. We have to invest time in anticipating answers but that could be at odds with the point above.   2

That means we need some quality control checks, on ourselves! We should make sure we do just-in-time QA checks on ourselves!   3

This is going to top out at two day work units so we need to automate things like the analysis, which means giving more care and attention to questions.   4

We want to propagate it online so we need some smart thinking about how to get a quick reaction on Twitter. But we have never used social media like this before.

We also want the potential to gamify filling out the survey as that often works better than incentives.

You can see that there is scope here to add in new goals, like gamification. That might be something we do as we move the analysis of work further. Critically, the ambition to work in two day units is driving this. It is possible to take a month over a questionnaire design but once you say it has to be done in two days then you have to think harder about what matters, what has value.

We came up with this short list below in just under half an hour.

Scope of questions: draft 1

Background:
For automated analysis Q has to be multiple choice.... 1 - 5

Need to be wary of ambiguity in scoring mechanism

Set one question that gives us their boundaries: are they a 3 type person or a 5 type person, ie always scoring middle or always scoring high.

Design analysis to reweight scores based on that.

Cover:
Emotional experience of distributorship
Practical experiences
    Journey to
    Journey from
Trust factors
    Comfort
    Pricing
    Transparency
Attitudinal
    Perceived value of warranty
    Attitude to transport issues
    Perceptions of residual value of car

A set of priorities like that needs to be iterated with what we expect the answers might be. That's not to say you shape the questionnaire to get certain answers. But you have to frame questions so that the responses are not useless. You need a rough idea of what value those answers will have for you. The key term, of course, is iterated. We won't get it right the first time. And these thoughts can go up on a wall for other people to comment on. Are the likely outcomes suggesting actions in line with our goals or do they suggest new goals?

As this iterative process evolves, the initial matrix can be expressed as a set of statements on Post-Its, as is traditional in Agile. The only reason we have not done so here is that the format is difficult to reproduce in a book. The Post-Its could say things like:

1. As the Flow value manager I want to organise consensus on the most valuable outcomes of an online survey.

2. I need a draft list of questions to ask customers in the online survey.

    a. I need to devise categories for the questions and describe potential outcomes that the answers will yield (I might feel this is too big a challenge to work on in isolation).

    b. I need to organise a standup to socialise the draft.

    c. I need to decide on open-ended or multiple choice or both.

3. As an analyst I need to assess and choose survey tools.

    a. And I really need feedback and input on the choice of tool.

    b. I also need to convert the draft into a survey using the chosen tool.

    c. And I need to help pilot the survey

4. As a Flow value manager I need an evaluation of instant communications for the survey: Twitter, WhatsApp, Telegram etc.

5. As a social media expert I need to figure out how to propagate the survey online and provide that review of the state of the art to the Flow value manager.

And so on. These tasks can be codesigned in a short meeting. They can clearly be broken down further to get to a shorter cycle-time. Once they are posted on a project board, everybody knows what's going on, what needs to be done, how the work is going to get done (none of these tasks are going to go on for more than two days), and why. All this can go onto the Post-It and the board.

It's a good idea also to keep reminding yourself that the goals are an important source of discipline.

There is still some work to do here in breaking the work down into more discrete tasks that could then be transferred to a team Kanban board with the Work to do: In Progress: Completed, structure.

Because each of the goals and task areas is visible to everybody, anybody can raise questions about the value of a unit of work. In particular developers are empowered to do that. This is critical to the new team dynamic. Business value is not assumed simply because there is a request to do work.

INTRODUCING CONTINUOUS INNOVATION

You may be familiar with Continuous Improvement, Continuous Learning or indeed Continuous Delivery and all of these topics feature heavily in Flow. They are integral to the new capabilities of IT. They are the ideas that are now spreading out across the organisation.

However, introducing the topic of Continuous Innovation re-quires a moment or two for reflection in order to fully understand the conditions that fuel such a concept. Trust and belief are central to it.

THE DICTIONARY DEFINITION OF TRUST

Noun: Firm belief in the reliability, truth or ability of something or someone.

When there is no trust in a team, then fear and anxiety are kings. They feed on each other. They create a domino effect that impacts everyone. It creates an enterprise dystopia where people spend more time complaining about each other than they do seeking value.

You may have worked in a low trust environment and noted the culture: It's survival of the fittest or strongest or most Machiavellian. Many people can survive it because they have had to. That's the way the workplace has been. What is saddening though is the psychic impact on team members and ultimately the loss of opportunity to drive valuable business outcomes.

If team members have a leader that they can trust and that person is one of many leaders who openly demonstrate mutual respect, ideas and innovation will grow. The atmosphere becomes exhilarating, intoxicating, even positively disruptive.

Sounds a bit like a well-run start-up. Or a really culturally aware organisation. Creating a safe environment (in particular a no blame culture) means enabling team members to be bold & brave enough to learn from their mistakes. This is part of what takes the organisation beyond continuous improvement to continuous innovation.

And that sometimes means, well in fact quite often means, acknowledging that "the culture" of an organisation is really about people, emotions, trust and belief.

Dealing with these emotions is usually termed "soft skills" but in fact they are the toughest challenge you can take on. The leader, at whatever level of the company, has to care about everyone's "psychic income" or emotional rewards. If this concern doesn't come naturally then you will not be a good manager. Many leaders cannot take this step. They can't bring themselves to care about employee income broadly defined and they need to move on to another company - assuming you want a high trust culture to develop. Reflection on trust over. Now we turn to methodologies.

THE EVOLUTION OF METHODOLOGIES

When Fin talks about Flow he starts with the evolution of methodologies and the amount of effort required in order to gain value from a project or initiative within different work settings.

Back in the day, Waterfall was the only software methodology available. It wasn't uncommon to have projects spanning multiple years tying up resources until a delivery was completed. Only then could value be properly assessed.

Reflect for a minute. You could only really be sure of value once you had spent a huge amount of cash and killed a lot of time. Very likely a lot of that cash was tied up in putting right many of the mistakes, collisions and misunderstandings that arise with big projects. It was not spent on value. These were the days when software platforms really began to shape the way people worked across the organisation. We're thinking ERP and systems like Sharepoint that dominated business culture for two decades.

In the development of these systems there was no scope for deviation or pivoting, not for those creating them or those implementing them or those using them. Sadly they also took their toll on organisational culture because they defined how people had to work. The software became your boss.

We are now escaping that era. The old IT department used Waterfall methods following the project management methods derived from large military projects and the construction industry. Software methodology was modelled on environments where there were very real critical paths and dependencies. It is absolutely true that you cannot pour concrete foundations without first digging trenches. But the modern workplace does not need that sequential logic. It is perfectly feasible, acceptable and good to start a project just about anywhere.

Beginning by thinking about a user interface before a line of code is written is a good thing. Drafting a few features to include in a matrix to test with users is good. There is no critical path to it. Critical paths and dependencies do exist but they are not the defining structure of work that they are in Waterfall and Agile.

The project management approach sees all work in terms of a logical beginning (the plan) and end (project completion) with a lot of milestones and deliverables in between. In contrast, the modern workplace is, well, a continuous work-in-progress.

The first signs of improvement came when organisations began to see Agile as an alternative. Getting high quality software out-the-door quickly has been the mantra of Agile for quite some time and Scrum has helped. But what happened? Scrum became frozen in time as consultants focused on activities like certification and enterprise level frameworks. This latter is almost a return to Waterfall. In principle Agile is great. In practice it has not been able to shake off its roots in project management and the methods designed for entirely different industries and applications.

Like Waterfall before it, many implementations of Scrum now tie up resources for long periods of time (weeks & months) before value can be delivered (or to discover whether a project will be successful or fail). Of course weeks is faster than years but very often real value in Scrum only emerges after multiple sprints (in other words months, after all).

Many Agile practitioners decided that something had to change and looked to Kanban as a way forward. Kanban has similar ceremonies to Scrum but it favours more collaboration, limits the work in progress and hates waste - especially teams having to wait for each other or having to dedicate whole sprints to fixing bugs that arise when multiple teams merge their code together.

That situation is rife with conflict but worse it imperils the organisation. Business gets stuck. Innovation is stalled. People start to blame each other. IT is not seen as a medium for change. It is perceived as the enemy.

However, we are moving to a situation where Kanban, coupled with work breakdown and continuous delivery techniques, delivers code so quickly that merging or branching code is not required. Teams don't collide with each other.

This is so important for the rest of the business. It means that the role of software as an enabler is coming good. Flow is the next logical step. In most enterprises we seek a continuing relationship with customers, derived from multiple layers of features, services, products and functions. There is no beginning, middle and end. Innovation flows like a deep river. One key to it is reduced cycle-time.

AN EASIER WAY TO WORK FASTER FOR MORE VALUE

Most engineers think of reducing cycle-time to, say, two or three weeks or longer. That's about the length of a Scrum-Agile sprint. However we talk about cycle-time in terms of days. Preferably two days at most. And we think this is applicable in all areas of the business, not just IT.

There are so many reasons why this is beneficial. But here's an often overlooked one. Handled skillfully, shorter cycle-times make work more collaborative.

Imagine if colleagues produced valuable work every couple of days and work was organised so that colleagues would be telling you, the team or a leader, about that experience, that unit of work, that outcome, just two days after beginning the work.

That makes for a very interactive and social work environment and a very regular check-in on progress.

One reaction to that is it is like "checking up" on people. Too bad if you think that way. Checking in with colleagues and getting quick course-corrections is essential if you are not going to waste time later fixing what you got wrong.

Coupled to the Wall visualisations we talk about in Flow, people build a variety of venues to discuss innovation and the road to value. Even more exciting, they get to co-decide the direction a block of work-units might take.

With the introduction of Microservices and DevOps, continuous innovation is now a stark or exciting reality, depending on your viewpoint. In place of an innovation funnel that constantly rejects innovations at stage-gates, you now have a pipeline or flow that continuously tests new ideas between colleagues and with customers.

You need to have many, many decisions made in that flow, as close to the moment of go-live as possible. The key is to develop the right types of interaction, shaping all available knowledge, to ensure the decision-making is well-informed.

Short cycle-times encourage the *levels* of interaction that give you better decisions. Walls provide you with the venue. As we say, good decisions stem from good social interactions at work and that happens at the Walls.

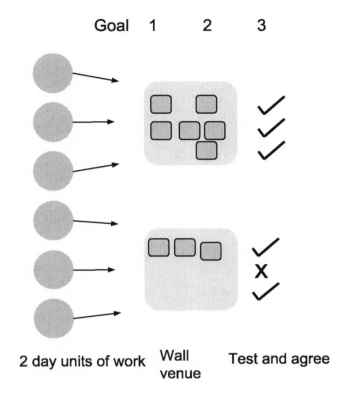

As well as good interaction, we have interaction with a purpose - the search for value. Let's rephrase this for the sake of clarity.

1.   We work in two day work units or shorter, directed by flexible business goals that give us a sense of the work's value.

2.   Those work units are what we collectively decide will be tasks that might create value for customers within the context of our business goals.

3.   After two days we interact around those work units. We can now query goals and confirm and adapt them.

4.   We decide if they should be pushed through to a collection of work units ready to show to customers (we call this a minimum sustainable delivery matrix (MSD).

5.   The MSD is pushed to a customer feedback environment.

6.   We learn about value and we iterate back to the work unit if elements of the MSD are shown to be weak or we enhance for a wider audience if they are shown to be strong (i.e. have value).

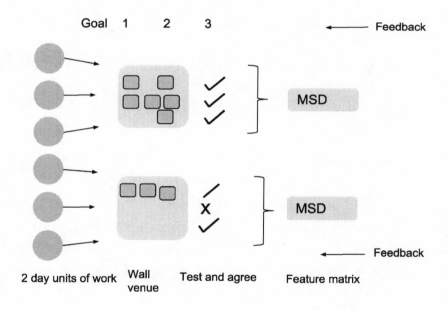

You can see a Customer Feedback Wall in Chapter 10. In this way of working is we are not writing Epics or User Stories, as in Agile. We are socialising the process of reaching flexible business goals (see Chapter 5) and using that as a framework for work breakdown.

There are such amazing benefits to be drawn from short cycle-times but to get there you need to commit to more social interaction, more visible work and new skills. In particular the interaction around work breakdown becomes a critical orchestrating event.

THE BENEFITS OF MINIMUM SUSTAINABLE DELIVERY (MSD)

We introduced the concept of MSD as a true alternative to MVP because we see multiple problems with MVPs. Sustainable delivery is all about:

1. Recognising that most companies now have a whole matrix of innovation on the go and that much of the work-in-progress is really about multiple innovations of many features.

2. Recognising that we have to get features and functions in front of end customers quickly and often, so we can see what value they really have. Everything else is theoretical. Theory is good but we need proof.

3. Highlighting the benefits of speed to feedback and getting a measure of value much faster.

4. Building upon this, understanding when an initiative is succeeding or failing as a key to informing the team whether to continue with work or to stop and pivot.

The work is driven by a value-seeking culture. Here's an example and a model for that. As we pointed out earlier, Sky cycling team, the most successful cycling team of the past decade, built their success around a concept called the aggregation of marginal gains. Their idea was to make small 1% improvements to everything they did in order to build towards the ultimate goal of winning the Tour de France.

Conversely, 1% declines in performance would demonstrate that something wasn't working, such as a dietary change or training plan. Sky's techniques helped it to become world beaters.

Flow works with similar principles. The aggregation of small deliveries will, for instance, show whether an initiative is making an improvement in sales and customer satisfaction or the opposite and it will do this long before a project-sized initiative would. Elsewhere, incremental gains have been described as a kind of options system. However, real options analysis is much more complex than we really have time for in today's innovation environment. We are talking about improvement rather than significant changes in direction.

When a team is immersed in Flow and great social interaction prevails over rules, teams crave the opportunity to improve their products or applications. The 1% gains are easy to come by and they are continuous.

Great leaders won't wait for a product manager to come up with a great idea. They will encourage the teams to collaborate so that they can generate more ideas and use Flow to test and learn with real customers.

If an idea flourishes, then the team can continue building. If it fails, then the team removes the code (leaving no technical debt) and then pivots. Flow teams don't build to perfection before testing with customers. We look for the minimum sustainable matrix of features to put in front of them.

What we also do is use Walls, such as Thank You Walls and Jobs Walls (see the book Flow), that develop mutual appreciation and respect in teams, the critical non-essentials in creating a culture of continuous innovation.

Taken together these two facets of work, continuous marginal improvements and Critical Non-essentials, give you the culture and work cadence that delivers more and more value. And the key channel for that is the minimum sustainable delivery matrix, those features you push out for feedback and refine quickly to optimise customer success. They mean your culture is built around proof points of value. They provide evidence to people that their work is good. And they let people appreciate the bold outcomes of good social interaction.

MORE ON WORKING FASTER

Choosing the correct methodology is key to reducing cycle-time and then being able to aggregate units of work for testing with customers.

It's a no-brainer that Waterfall has the longest cycle-time. That's why it has become so inappropriate. The moment when we might discover the value of a project is pushed too far into the future.

Planning ahead has also become increasingly difficult. And large units of work inevitably collide when the moment comes to integrate them. This is as true of marketing or logistics as it is of IT as software and digital work plays a more central role. This trend is one reason why companies are seeking to introduce formal Agile techniques in different areas of the business.

The reasons that Scrum fails, however, are somewhat similar to why Waterfall became inappropriate. Even three week sprints are too long and create their own collisions.

The Kanban techniques adopted in Flow limit work in progress (i.e. the amount of work coming into the funnel). The team only accepts tasks when there is someone available to work on them. That means that anything "not in play" can be continually refined by Business Analysts. The purpose of that is to ensure there is no confusion as to what's required of the next person to pick up the work - there is more dialogue around what is needed and what has value. Because more time is spent at the (work) breakdown, analysts get time to order the backlog (or inflow) of work in terms of its potential value to customers or what looks likely to create customer success most easily.

The organisation of work is gravitating to a situation where work can be divided between lead time and cycle-time. Each of these has revision points.

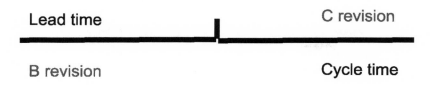

The business side of the team takes responsibility for the first part of the journey (let's call the tasks here "value identification & prioritising") and the tech team side of the time takes a higher profile during the cycle-time, which is when the development work takes place. Each of these segments of work seeks opportunities for revision either based on business priorities (B Revision) or customer feedback (C Revision).

Just this simple allocation of responsibility improves cycle-time because there is suddenly an emphasis on prioritisation for the whole team. Both are becoming value-seeking.

Other ways of reducing cycle-time are outlined in our first book on Flow. For instance, the technique SailBoat highlights inefficient processes; times when the team are waiting for something or someone and can't continue their work; or when teams have been pulled out of shape by excess demands on their time.

The discipline of value-seeking behaviour lies in having an external party or priority (the customer) who can guide teams in getting to value quickly.

We also use the 2 day cycle-time to prevent all kinds of rework and context switching. When a team member has to stop work on a task and start a new one because of a delay upstream, returning to the original task later is called context switching. In software development it is problematic because they usually can't remember the original work item when they return to it and they have to start over again. Similar situations arise in any content process too. Being able to break work down so that it can be executed in small steps allows people to complete a modules without interference.

Reducing context switching helps keep cycle-times under control. It also contributes to new team combinations. It didn't take a genius or an expert in the theory of constraints to see there has long been a serious bottleneck between the development and operations teams in IT departments or lately where marketing and IT intersect.

Creating holistic teams with the same framework of value helps overcome these divides. Flow advocates for holistic teams that bring the business and IT teams together at the same table. Some people are calling this BizDevOps or even BizDevSecOps. But you can clearly see that if you remove the handoffs between teams, cycle-times will improve. They improve more quickly when roles become more fungible.

We are big fans of fungible roles (T-shaped, Pi-shaped and Comb-shaped roles). These concepts are quite widely known. Their main advantage is that people can, and should, take on more tasks. They should not be as specialised as in the past.

If I as a developer think I need a digital business analyst to do some work on a problem, I could stop and ask why not do it myself? As a marketer could I not learn how to specify a request for development work that shows some insight into how IT functions? Why do I need a business analyst to do this?

The last component of reducing cycle-time is automation. This is a very IT-centric issue but if IT gets this right then the business can take advantage of reduced cycle-time, faster feature releases and more opportunity to test with customers.

The benefit to the business is that them more we can abstract away the complexities of the infrastructure, the more cycle-time will be reduced and the better it is for the people who need to test new features with customers. Of course the business needs to know about these new capabilities what new opportunities they open up. Collectively we spend too little time discussing that.

NEW WAYS OF WORK (OH WOW!!)

Now think about your cycle-time reduction pilot as your own internal requirement to create new ways of working.

Here are some of the benefits you need to be targeting as you prototype your own process model innovations, building out Flow as a new way of working. You need to toggle between Chapter 5 and here, in order to get this right! Here is a mini-12 step rationale and approach to get to cycle-time reduction.

1.   Smaller work units foster more interaction, they also make it less likely that teams will create outputs that are incompatible with the work of other teams and make it less likely that they will have strayed away from the objectives of the overall project.

2.   More interaction makes it possible for people to codesign the best way to meet business goals. Most people these days need to do some multidisciplinary work and an important aspect of this is for IT and the business to work closely together. All disciplines can feel more confident that work is meeting their goals if they work together on it.

3.   Teams can function in a multidisciplinary environment if they are able to observe work - without observable work it is impossible, say, for IT to pivot where necessary, because IT will need to take the business along on that pivot. Two to three week cycles times inhibit interdisciplinary deci-

sion making and so too does the culture of deliverables and tradition of reports.

4. More interaction allows new tools, techniques and work-arounds to come to the surface and inform solution design.

5. Shorter cycle-times make budgeting much more intuitive. A work unit is 2 days of a developer's time so a hundred units of work is equal to 200 work days. Because all work is visible, budgeting is there on the wall, at a glance.

6. Visible work makes it possible to see dependencies and risks over time. No longer do you need a genius who can go away and anticipate all dependencies and all risk factors. People can add them in as they see them, as the work is broken down.

7. That also makes it easier to overcome work allocation problems. If someone is off sick, the gap can be plugged if the dependency and risk is high, or otherwise it can be left until that person is back.

8. Many hands make light work - especially of difficult creative tasks. No single brain can manage work planning in complex environments where innovation is continuous. The group has to shape the knowledge flow that makes good work possible. Flow is all about collective intelligence.

9. The process of work breakdown is, by its nature, a group task. While there are people who naturally want to lead work breakdown, it needs good domain expertise to shape it properly; it needs business to specify goals; and it needs interaction to keep goals relevant.

10. The value of work is more easily visible if the work unit is small. Either it adds value to a package of features that are being pushed to customers or it doesn't and it is dropped.

11. Time to feedback is shortened too. That means teams can develop prototype features and compile these into what we call a minimum sustainable delivery package that can go live to customer groups for A/B testing and other feedback mechanisms.

12. Small work units make it possible to pivot at short notice. No-one gets over invested in any particular piece of work. if it doesn't add value to customer experiences, it's dropped and the cost of testing an idea is kept low.

We are going to cover all these points again later in more detail and in a different context, so don't worry too much if they don't sink in first time around. Rome wasn't built in a day.

CHAPTER 4

Taking Advantage of Visible Work

Speaking recently to a client implementing Flow, he asked: "I am thinking of introducing an Accomplishments Wall. The one thing we don't do enough of here is take the time and trouble to pat ourselves on the back or mark an occasion when we achieve something. What do you think?" What we think is that Flow belongs to everybody. Having Walls that support people's emotions is crucial. It is a critical non-essential, so go with it.

In this chapter we are going to look at how to introduce such visible, or observable, work. It is a keystone for a new organisational culture. In this culture, collective intelligence plays an important part in shaping knowledge. In matrix innovation, the need for judgments and decisions is vastly multiplied and very granular. The decision points need to be there for everybody to see.

Information is also super-abundant so bringing judgments to bear on decisions means shaping large knowledge flows. The Wall visualisations allow everybody to see the decision points and to play a role in shaping responses based on their part of the know-how. That can be their tidbits from meetups or insights from prior work, their reading or tools they have used before. Social interaction shapes knowledge and supports decisions.

How do you go about creating a visual work culture? Just as important, if you have hundreds of work units, does this create too much complexity?

The answer is three-fold. First, work is more complex anyway. That's a fact of life. Second, complexity can be more easily managed through the collective intelligence of good teams than it can with hierarchies and plans. Third, Walls can be used to support people (for example Appreciation Walls that allow colleagues to say thanks!).

On the first of these, when the electronics giant Samsung set out to create an Active Matrix Organic Light Emitting Diode (AMOLED) screen for smartphones they hired Russian TRIZ masters to help organise and inspire people. The TRIZ method looks at a project like "create an AMOLED screen for the first time" as a set of problem statements, a bit like our units of work.

Their main mission was to create a screen that would not need a backlight and therefore could be flexible. Mission two was to create a screen that could potentially offer far better colour saturation than LCD (the type of display used by Apple). They divided these two goals into 50 major problem areas such as the science of phosphor-based diodes and the challenges of large-scale production of AMOLED.

These challenges were then divided into hundreds of problem statements, making in total thousands of problems (think of these as goals) that needed a solution. It worked! Samsung dominates the AMOLED display industry.

Flow is analogous. The search for value comes down to many small steps we can take to solve problems, just like AMOLED. Instead of problem statements we use goals to direct the construction of areas of work and units of work.

On the second point, dealing in hundreds of small steps in an environment that is highly visual and interactive is much simpler than creating a grand plan and then trying to corral dozens of people to deliver it, all the while hoping the plan stays relevant.

Very often people see the promised value of a plan unravelling before their eyes. Maybe the planning was poor or reality changes as the project unfolds. People become disengaged because they realise they are creating a dud; or they get frustrated by the complexity of merging separate strands of a project whose parts vary in quality.

Visualisation and social interaction are a big contrast to this. Flow is based on an explicit acknowledgement of complexity and *therefore* the need to codesign the best way to solve multiple challenges. Visualisation and smaller units of work are effective tools for it. They don't have a huge book of rules around them. Flow is a light framework after all. But what it really means is that people are trusted to design the right process and solution. That's another way of saying they are empowered.

The third point we made is that visualisation allows people to develop their own, rich culture of interaction and support. We already gave an example of that at the start of the chapter, a client who felt his journey should begin with an Accomplishments Wall. Great. Start with the emotions.

We often overlook the fact that many people have emotional intelligence but lack emotional resilience. They duck and dive the corporate politics. But they often lack resilience to stand up for ideas they believe in. They bend too easily. By visualising work processes and emotions we can elicit ideas from introverted people and support them in joining the change. With visualisation:

- Work can be observed and therefore more people can contribute to the design of solutions and the appropriate flow - we get the benefit of collective intelligence.

- Work matures over time in place of large planning sessions that try to second-guess the development of a project over its lifespan.

- The Walls can be venues for all kinds of discussions about where value lies and how to get there.

- More risks and issues can be exposed.

- People interact around decisions.

- Being visible helps document the organisation's learning and learning accumulates. People share ideas in asynchronous as well as synchronous ways. The walls of the building become alive with what you are doing, what you are sharing and what you are learning.

VISIBLE WORK

The visible work movement, or what was sometimes referred to as Observable Work, dates back to the mid to late-2000s. Perhaps it is too much to call it a movement, yet. Nonetheless, a small debate began and people like Jim McGee and Greg Lloyd pitched in on its importance. While McGee was writing in 2010, he had initiated this discussion as early as 2002.

It's worth quoting him:

As a knowledge worker, much of what I get paid for happens inside my own head. Before the advent of a more or less ubiquitous digital environment, however, that head work used to generate a variety of markers and visible manifestations.

He pointed out that the "visible manifestations" had the advantage of allowing people to observe work-in-progress and get a sense of how well-baked a set of ideas might be.

We particularly like McGee's observation that work has become "invisible" and therefore harder to manage. Much of what we do has disappeared into the laptop. Gains in personal productivity, as he puts it, have been acquired at the expense of organisational learning. Along with that, interaction has dried up and the essence of knowledge-work has been lost. What is that essence?

It is something that we point out in Flow. The essence of knowledge work, especially right now, is that most of what we do is brand new. We have little opportunity to copy work done earlier or rely on repetition.

And we work in an environment where information is overabundant. Our challenge goes beyond the fact that work is not being socialised. There is just too much novelty out there. We cannot manage the superabundance of matrix innovation without total support.

Two things emerged from the visible work debate:

1.   It was generally accepted that software development had advanced the cause of visible or observable work more than any other section of the knowledge economy. The concepts of version tracking, iterative development and output testing, at least offered up a flow of visible, shared experience.

2.   New tools, like feeds, were making some elements of work more visible. However, they were visible only in the sense that conversations about work were available in a feed or a stream. Real human interaction was still very limited.

At the same time, software developers were beginning to use more visible techniques borrowed from Lean and Kanban. Agile teams began using Post-Its to walk through any given problem or to represent the major Epics and Stories that lie at the heart of their discipline. Having said there was more visualisation was there a real gain in social interaction?

VISIBLE WORK AND SOCIAL INTERACTION

Knowledge work is commonplace now. It relies on smart people sharing ideas, background information, news and know-how. This knowledge needs to accumulate and become true organisational learning. Organisations in the past were not under the same pressure they are to deliver multiple streams of innovation simultaneously.

Every firm, and any public agency, is faced with trying to make sense of AI/ML IoT, Blockchain, disintermediation caused by business platforms, continuous delivery, new patterns of global trade, global cash oversight, complex supply chains, new business ecosystems, and heightened political risk.

The organisation is also more porous and will become even more so. As companies become more familiar and experienced at working with ecosystems, we anticipate more use of micro-outsourcing (the use of small contracts to fulfil part of a development or marketing program), ecosystems and other small company relationships

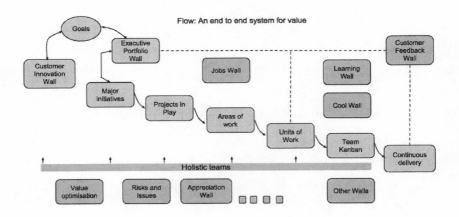

Flow: An end to end system for value

The challenges with introducing extreme visualisation are not so great as to be a serious inhibitor. Nonetheless they need looking at. But we suggest you do that in the context of a Flow Circle. In other words, within the context of a positive attempt to consider how you will launch extreme work visibility and improved social interaction. The diagram above is a simplified version of Flow in practice that shows an extreme form of visual representation. All these visualisations are venues for social interaction.

Here are a few examples of Flow Walls in action. In the first book we list about 15 that would form part of a coherent approach to continuous innovation. Below you see a work breakdown wall (or Project Wall), an Appreciation Wall, and a Feasibility Wall. These three are just a sample.

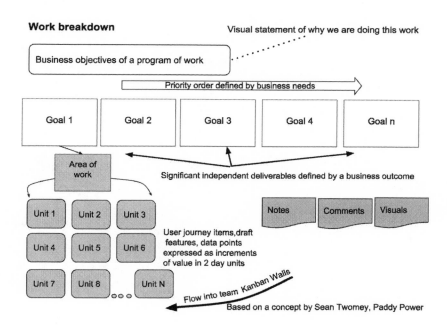

INTRODUCING EXTREME VISUALISATION

The simple steps and inhibitors to beginning visible work are:

1. **SPACE.** Do you have sufficient Wall Space? In Paddy
    Power, an early Flow advocate, one of the most important

walls is in the corridor. It's there because everybody has to walk past it. Everybody has to see it. To do good visible work you need a lot of wall space or you need to be willing to use dividers that will be permanently in place (i.e. will not be borrowed by other teams). Whiteboards can be a useful place to start, but they will get wiped! If you start by using whiteboards, remember to take photos of each stage of a visible project. Most importantly don't use a meeting room. You need somewhere public.

2. **ANTICIPATING RESISTANCE.** We have recommended elsewhere that the places to begin are the Customer Wall or the Executive Portfolio Wall.

It can be difficult to coax executives into doing visible work. More than any other part of the organisation, members of the executive suite prefer to sustain mystery around their decision making. We'll say more about that in a later step.

The Customer Wall gives you a chance to play to the needs of the organisation - you need to segment customers better, you need to discuss customer goals and customer access, you need to make customer feedback visible etc. All these point to Customer Walls being an area less likely to meet resistance.

3. **ADAPTATION.** Given that most organisations will be using some form of visualisation, it pays to roll an extreme visualisation program into that or vice versa. It might be that you have a pressing project and that can be the focal point for beginning extreme visibility. Great. Go for it. That's what we talked about when interviewing Sean

Twomey at Paddy Power. Sean gives a great account of how they invented short cycle-times and what it takes to get there - it is essential reading alongside this and you will find it in Chapter 5.

4.   **RESEARCH.** Customer Walls need some social media research or research in the call-centre files if they are to be effective. This is a good thing. Making a decision in a Flow circle to commission a small amount of research on segmentation or feedback gives you data, and data shows you're not just there to pass the time of day. And it gives you the opportunity to share new information publicly. The data will go up on the wall.

Equally if the decision is to go with an Executive Portfolio Wall, you need to collate data on all the projects in play. There is more on both of these steps later in the book.

5.   **THE FIRST DRAFT.** Doing visible work is a bit like hanging up the washing. People see things you might like to keep hidden or, just as uncomfortable, you and your colleagues will struggle to get a session working well right off the bat. It takes experience to do Walls like Customer and Executive.

Now, that experience can be bought in for the day in the shape of a facilitator. But it also resides in your team. The person that likes to anticipate. Yes, the one who is quite thoughtful and can work through the session ahead of time to see the pitfalls and then figure out how to bring people together....

She's the one who should hold the markers and take the lead. For sure, don't let an actual leader become too prominent. People will hang back and wait to be led.

6.   **REPORTING.** Resist the temptation to write this project or process up. If you need to write something up it defeats the point. Whatever you arrive at, it is there on the wall. If you delegate a write-up task to someone then everything will go into a laptop and, worse, you will get one person's interpretation of what happened. Keep it live. Use photos not reports.

7.   **TOOLS TO HAVE TO HAND.** To be effective there is some preparation. It pays to already be thinking about a Learning Wall.

• **THE LEARNING WALL.** All that means at this stage is a sacred space that you can use to document what you are learning from this process.

• **A GO TO MARKET PLAN.** Most development work really needs to be couched within a GO-To-MARKET plan or a template that the firm recognises as a valid and disciplined way to think about the market when you are creating products or services. We've sketched out a GTM template in our first book.

• **PLENTY OF POST-ITS AND MARKERS**

• **A CAMERA.** A smartphone is good enough but document and share what you are doing and do it visually. The reason for this is not just that we habitually take photos these days. Having a visual record will allow you to resist the temptation to write it up.

CHAPTER 5

Anti-Project Thinking and Business Agility

In this chapter we want to argue that Agile techniques could be improved by moving away from *Epics* and *User Stories* to *Flexible Business Goals, Areas of Work and Units of Work*. We will also argue that many project management techniques get in the way of agility.

The reason is that technology and market dynamics have changed the workplace. We are now dealing with multiple intangible assets: relationships with customers that are built through trust-management techniques and service quality; digital assets that are given away; vast catalogues of options that customers can take, hence multiple interfaces presenting different messages or incentives; data that comes from dozens of sources; communications that range across hundreds of outlets (not just TV, print and outdoor but also via the imprimatur of a customer segment's favourite YouTube star, a friend's Instagram page or an influencer).

Set alongside this, most companies face the prospect of doing multiple new things all the time (AI, blockchain, IoT, etc). Earlier, we referred to this as "atomisation", the fragmentation of old value-chains into hundreds of inter-related units of work that make up matrix-innovation. Traditional and agile ways of work cannot cope with this level of novelty because they are built on replicability (having done tasks dozens of times).

We need new ways to work. We'll discuss that in the context of Paddy Power Betfair where may features of Flow originated. Paddy Power Betfair is an online betting site that initiated a completely new system of open, visual and collaborative work design from 2012 onwards as it prepared to become a mobile-first company.

The performance of this relatively small Dublin based company compares favourably with many of the global Internet giants. It serves more than 3.5 billion application program interface (API) requests every day—a number similar to Netflix, eBay, Facebook, or Twitter, according to infrastructure provider RedHat. It handles around 130 million transactions daily—more than 10 times the number of daily transactions at the London Stock Exchange. These levels of performance are supported by the Flow philosophy, one part of which is to reject project management.

One of the lessons from Paddy Power and other implementations of Flow is the need to prioritise goals over Epics and User Stories.

Goals are flexible statements of what a good outcome of work should look like. We break goals down into areas of work and then units of work each with its own goals. If, in practice, a good outcome does not look likely to emerge, or early tests show it to be built on a false assumption or it lies too far in the distance, the goal can change and work can be redesigned so it continues to be of value. In other words, the goal can change and teams can switch to units of work that create value more quickly.

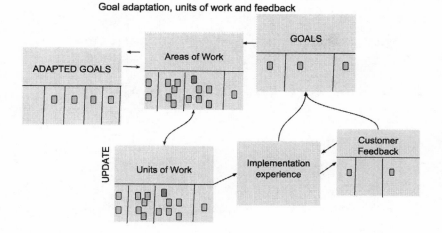

Goal adaptation, units of work and feedback

These techniques and the relationships that go with them (all work is visual and interactive) epitomise the *business agile* mindset. They apply to all areas of the business.

As an illustration of the broader picture, when social media began around 2007, marketers, inspired by bloggers who were completely immersed in new ways of writing, had to find ways to channel brand messages through the canals and by-ways of blogging's personal form of communications. They had to learn search engine optimisation. And adapt to Google, and Google Analytics and then to Facebook Twitter, Instagram and Snapchat.

Many companies got the etiquette of digital communications completely wrong and some still do. They lacked in-house skills because they outsourced all of their branding and communications to agencies!

Those who were prepared to explore new ways of work (what Fin happily calls the WOW effect!!), discovered new processes and a new sensibility to authentic communications that they will now have extended to Snapchat, Instagram, Pinterest and so on.

All work is becoming less monolithic and more atomised. This atomisation of work needs to be embraced. We need to build new frameworks to support people in designing and doing smaller units of work.

BECOMING ANTI-PROJECT

To get in the flow you need to reject traditional project management techniques. Project management thinking dominates most areas of work. The core ideas of milestones, dependencies and deliverables create a rigid structure that prevents teams from questioning value or adapting to circumstances. Projects are there to be completed not queried.

Project management is so ingrained that people think of it as a natural way to work. Yet it is the most artificial and over-articulated of all work methods. In traditional project management, planners use a work breakdown structure (WBS) to organise work (this structure is baked into many project management software tools). Here's how that is defined:

> A **work-breakdown structure (WBS)**, also referred to as "Contract Work Breakdown Structure " or "CWBS,"[1] in project management and systems engineering, is a deliverable-oriented breakdown of a project into smaller components. A work breakdown structure is a key project deliverable that organizes the team's work into manageable sections. The Project Management Body of Knowledge(PMBOK 5) defines the work breakdown structure as a "A hierarchical decomposition of the total scope of work to be carried out by the project team to accomplish the project objectives and create the required deliverables."

These ideas stem from the US Department of Defence and US Navy from the 1950s. Don't know about you but we doubt we could enjoy working in that type of environment. For some years one of us worked with technology projects that followed a similar template. Work packages, divided into activities and tasks, all with milestones and deliverables attached. Nothing could be more stultifying, especially when you are trying to define (and budget) all that before writing a line of code or writing a word of copy.

These procedures have had an enormous influence on how projects are planned, executed and reported. They influenced the old way of doing software, the Waterfall method. Waterfall projects were enormous pre-planned schedules of hierarchically designed work.

Agile principles were reasonably successful at undermining some of these structures. In some critical sense though Agile practices have changed the language without changing the behaviour. In Agile, projects are broken down into Epics and Stories, which is surely a project hierarchy by another name. And in Scrum these Epics and Stories are delivered in Sprints that come together in periodic Scrums. They are supervised by Scrum Masters (reminiscent to us of gang masters!).

Sprints are shorter cycles of work than would typically be found in a Waterfall project. But sprints cause their own problems, typically because teams develop their part of a project in the way they see fit, only to find it collides with what other people are doing! It needs rework and causes more delay. People go off and do other tasks while they wait and the chop and change culture this creates leads to more problems.

Epics and Stories present another difficulty. They rarely integrate customers into the process of work definition (the product owners becomes a stand-in for customers). They are limited as a way of defining what work really has value.

These are the shortcomings we try to address with Flow but we have to say Flow goes beyond just rectifying weaknesses in Agile. It has a totally different cultural perspective centred on interaction and collective intelligence.

We are anti-project and to some degree anti-plan because we don't believe these techniques answer today's work needs.

Formal project management techniques make more sense when they are applied to projects with physical materials and multiple parties involved. If you have a construction project where certain components, like concrete, underfloor plumbing, aggregate, electrical conduits and so on, all have to be delivered, then you have a very tight set of dependencies and a clear critical path. It would be foolish not to set these out. On the other hand, those dependencies and the critical path don't change much from project to project. Once set out they only need adapting. Formal project management techniques in these environments make sense.

Where products are intangible, we have a very different set of problems. In online betting or in insurance or, say, book sales or increasingly in any area of service that may or may not have a tangible product, the challenge has to be redefined

In the array of service possibilities that modern technology and service architecture opens up, and taking account of the desire of customers to have services and products tailored precisely to their needs, how can we create a consistent flow of innovations that adds to customers' success and builds their appreciation of us in a sustainable way (economically, environmentally and morally)?

In these situations we are not waiting on materials being supplied to us and nor are any of the dependencies so tight. All units of work have some connection with others but it is rare for the progress of one piece of work to absolutely prevent other units from starting. The critical path is not a big bold line.

In the modern workplace we want to codesign the right way to solve a problem; we can state goals; define work areas that help us refine goals; and break that into units of work. We have experience; we have a constant flow of information (customer data, customer feedback, new tools and techniques, case studies, everybody's past projects) and we have the possibility to create new team dynamics through visualisation. We transfer responsibility away from preset processes towards people seeking value. In other words we prioritise value-seeking behaviour in an environment where goals and work codesign rule.

Many formal project management techniques, even those of Agile, can kill the pursuit of value in favour of completing tasks and fulfilling roles. Flow is…. Well, fluid.

NOT MVP AND NOT LEAN

Over the past few years there has been quite a surge in interest in Lean principles as well as concepts such as minimum viable product (MVP). In the Eric Ries book Lean Startup, and in the writings of Steve Blank, there is a lot of good sense written about how entrepreneurs should function. But there's also a lack of understanding of how some large enterprises function.

There is an assumption that by osmosis large corporations will absorb these ideas and act in a startup kind of way. But being realistic for a second, 95% of technology startups fail. And nobody has really managed to nail down what makes the other 5% so vastly different. It is something to do with personality and resource management, the quality of an idea or invention, a bit of dog in the founder.

Assuming we know how startups really work is a risky attitude for large enterprises. As Fin pointed out recently, large companies are only intermittently in the position of seeking brand-new customers for a brand-new product. They have customers, they have a huge amount of work-in- progress, they have to introduce new technologies, and they will probably have some form of transformation program going. Introducing ideas like MVP to this environment can cause a host of issues:

- People have different ideas of what an MVP means. Sure, it is well defined by its proponents but in practice one person's MVP is another person's finished product. The idea of a "minimum" viable product makes business people tetchy as it signals to them that IT will only deliver a minimal amount of effort.

- That misunderstanding leads people to over-specify products in the hope that they can force IT to increase the "minimum" effort.

- This leads to long build times and elongated time to customer-feedback, in the process delaying time to value.

- What goes along with that is wasted infrastructure effort because IT has to build out new infrastructure, just-in-case an MVP development comes good.

- It also means lost opportunity as teams overlook value and instead focus on completion and delivery of an initial requirement.

The key is to keep work fluid - hence Flow. It means accepting fewer rules and processes and fewer boundaries in work structures. However, the minute you accept that you can take away rules you have to rely on the talent and commitment of the people who do the work. You have to accept that you have given them power over success and failure, hence the term empowerment.

The chief issue again comes down to fluidity. Projects can have a beginning, middle and end, with budgets, predefined outcomes and workflow or they can have those elements in an iteration cycle. But all these tools tempt you to see completion as the goal. Value is the goal. And in this new world completion is a rarity. Innovation is continuous.

The key is:

- Focus instead on business goals and ensure these represent real value.

- Train people to keep those goals flexible so that as you acquire more knowledge of customer needs, you can adapt the goals.

- Plan whatever units of work it takes to deliver the goals but do it in short bursts so that you can keep checking in with customers and colleagues.

- Be ready for multiple, micro-pivots as you create a matrix of features to put in front of customers.

This boundless form of working requires new techniques and one of the most important is to recompose the work hierarchy.

WORK BREAKDOWN IS YOUR BEST FRIEND

A lot of what is good in Flow rests on how good the work breakdown is. Work breakdown is one element of the Wall visualisations we referred to in the Handbook. What goes on the Wall matters deeply to work design.

Most work environments are built on the assumption that if you do the same task often enough you become really good at it. You might be bored out of your mind but you have a certain kind of expertise. That expertise might even help you think of new ways to perform your tasks. In a way, you would be an innovator.

The problem with that formula today is the sheer volume of new things we have to do. There isn't the opportunity to set up a sequence where people get to do the same thing repetitively and then hand on to the next person. Nor do we get the chance to iterate in a lean cycle. We need people to invent and we need them to do it dozens of times a week.

1.   Most things we are being asked to do are being done for the first time, e.g. using drones; introducing blockchain, AI, IoT. social media marketing via Snapchat stories, trading outside our core currencies and keeping track of digital revenues across the globe.

2.   Most of these require us to invent the process as well as the features, products or services even if only to adapt existing products and infrastructure to the digital age, for example via Cloud Migration.

3.   Knowing which features or services add value for customers is not easy and nor is it a given that even if requested by customers it will actually add value. Creating and adding value are steps that need some new sensibilities.

4.   Plus traditional handovers, the way we usually work, typically introduce errors and time wasting so handovers need to be eliminated.

We argue that an important feature of breaking work down, so that you see value and add it to the process, is the quality of social interaction that goes with a much shorter cycle-time. Shorter cycle-times force people to interact more. No more hiding in the warren of cubicles!

To get to the bottom of really good work breakdown…. Well that's why we spoke with Sean Twomey.

"Flow started for us," Sean explains, *"when we had a requirement for a new platform and a very short deadline. We had about three months over the summer to get something really significant done. But it was clear we weren't going to meet all of the business objectives set out for us.*

That put us in a position where we had to make critical decisions about what actually to do. And we had to act fast.

We drew out on one of the walls everything that we felt had to be built, at a high level, which led to mapping up a series of goals, each of which represented a significant independent deliverable to achieve a business outcome. That meant what we were doing was very visual. Being visual facilitated some decision making, which we needed because we couldn't achieve everything asked of us. By getting it out there we could socialise it between us.

When we had the goals we began translating those into projects, loosely defined in the sense of being a series of work units rather than anything in a project management plan. We also started to do some work breakdown, specifically what we could achieve within a week so we didn't go wandering down blind alleys. We didn't try to break all the work down, but just enough to get us going and get us to some demos.

What was very powerful was that this visual, the goals and the initial breakdown of work, was something that every business analyst, developer, and tester had to walk past several times every day. It wasn't about a group of us doing this in isolation. Everybody could see it.

They could also see what was coming at them and they had a chance to contribute to it too. People don't always take that opportunity but it's there and it helps, especially if they see work that they have some experience of or know how to shape.

And that's what some like to do. For us, the wall evolved so that it became like a kind of a progress bar too.

The project nearest the door, where the developers went into the workspace, were the ones with the most detailed breakdowns. That's where they could note down their next tasks and take it in to get the work done.

Further along, the walls were really more freeform. We had some comments, notes, and diagrams up there, a few ideas but nothing that would bog us down.

What's interesting about that is we still try to hold off the work breakdown until late in the process. We don't want to be taking teams away from delivery. What we prefer to do is wait until we need to pitch the work to developers as "this is what's coming next." Join us and work it out, sort of thing.

Often that means you have to take decisions about how much to put into a feature. If you can't demo in a week [in Flow we now aim for two days or less] then you need to break the work down further. That means you have a better chance of seeing where the value lies.

If you are going to demo maybe you demo a minimum viable feature and only develop the enhanced feature the following week or later. Or in building the minimum viable feature you find it has no real value for customers so you can drop it."

From what Sean is saying you start to get the picture. Work becomes fluid. It is a set of interactions around how to break work down, how to identify value, going back to work breakdown if value is not clear, trying a feature but being able to drop it out if necessary, calling on developer groups to join sessions where the work breakdown affects them. Constantly aiming for a shorter cycle-time so that the interaction of ideas, work and value is out in front of everybody.

THE WORK BREAKDOWN PROCESS IN A NUTSHELL

Here's a summary of the process Sean is describing and how it relates to conventional work practices, before we move onto how people interact in Flow environments. It's important to stress that the interaction is all important. What we are giving you here are the practical steps but how people contribute their expertise is just as critical.

1. There is a pressing business objective.

2. It is described as a series of goals (in Agile these might be described as Epics but we are really talking about business outcomes).

3. The first significant social interaction is around which goals will deliver value first. This can be done on whiteboards or cards on a wall. It's a simple question with a complicated conversation - what can we do to get us to the most value in the shortest time? Quite different from conventional planning with its beginning, middle and end.

4. The goals deemed most significant are broken down into incremental deliverable work items, generally by imagining them as a user-journey or workflow steps, or the kind of requirements users are known to have or might have (and the "might" element can be tested quickly!).

5. These can be described as stories, as they are in Agile, but the formality of Agile user-stories is less important than capturing the value that users can acquire from the features of the product or service. Capturing value, perhaps though specification by example, is partly about understanding user needs but also it's iterative - you can easily discover that your best ideas, and the ones that have a sign-off, provide no value. Being alive to new opportunities for value is vitally important.

6. The later goals are left on the wall for people to assess and comment so that they brew in people's imagination

and are there for people with previous domain expertise to share some knowledge around.

7.   The work breakdowns become story cards for developers and testers

8.   Story cards are intended to be completed within a 3 - 5 day period with a demo as a proof point (in later versions of Flow we specify 1 or 2 days, with the outputs being bundled into a minimum sustainable delivery matrix - one that customers will reasonably engage with).

9.   Minimum viable features can be created to test value and overall fit with the project.

10. They may lead to enhanced features or they may lead to a feature being dropped

11.   Along the Walls all kinds of dependencies become apparent to people over time. Nobody can spot all project dependencies in a planning document but by having projects out in the open dependencies emerge and can help with work allocation.

AN EXAMPLE OF HIGH LEVEL GOALS

In the first book we describe some of this sequencing by referring to a business objective like: We want to use drones for inspecting insurance incidents in order to speed up claims processing, reduce cost and improve service. This is a very high level objective: Discovering how do we best make use of drones to achieve the advantages of speed.

Assume for the sake of illustration that we begin this analysis with five main business goals. It is very likely that as we think about it, the number of goals will grow. We illustrate that below. At this point in the exercise we are working with goals rather than areas of work or units of work. The objective is to understand as far as possible which goals will guide the work and, very importantly, which point to the earliest gains in terms of value.

We have deliberately extended the range of goals well beyond what the IT shop would look after. There need to be strategy walls that bring IT and the business together, especially with significant new projects. So in this particular case we are looking across the business.

We want to start with a statement of proposed value. Drones are going to speed up claims' processing and in so doing, improve service to all members of the value chain, probably at a lower unit cost.

To get the process underway we guess at a short list of major goals:

- Goal 1. Understanding the concept.

- Goal 2: Achieving some uplift in brand communications.

- Goal 3: Crafting a base station design.

- Goal 4: Designing communications protocols.

- Goal 5: Creating expertise in security issues.

These could be completely wrong or half right. It doesn't matter. The principle is to get a conversation going. You should always be trying to define a goal as a business outcome. It is easy to state goals but more tricky to frame them as a business value. Clearly at this stage they are not stated in ways where value is clear. They are in some cases technical outcomes. On security, for example, we will want more value-centric statements as we progress. Security is vital in many respects; it is unavoidable. But we should be asking where can it add value? How can we use it to differentiate and provide more than people expect?

GOAL 1. UNDERSTANDING THE CONCEPT.

The idea of drones in everyday commercial use is new to us. The first goal is to improve our conceptual grasp of how drones function and their long term value; that might also include work units such as:

1. Looking at case studies, for example of how drones were used during Hurricane Sandy (ideas for drone use from underwriting through to claims settlement proliferated during that Hurricane, which is a nice illustration of how weather disruption triggered very rapid business disruption).

2. Potential benefits in reducing process handovers.

3. Understanding commercial drone specifications and flight laws.

4. Looking at specific requirements of drone use in insurance.

5. Seeking out sources of supply based on performance needs.

6. Testing or validating operational models.

7. Simultaneously setting out a business case for particular types of drone:

   - A cost benefit analysis that helps identify use-case specifications.

   - The cost of overcoming security risks.

   - Any examples of drone use that would help understand communications protocols.

   - And so on.

You can see from this initial breakdown that other business goals quickly become apparent and can be the framework for the next level of work breakdown (if you look back at Flow you will see we also make the point that all work breakdown can carry information, say colour codes or T Shirt sizes for scale of work unit or work area and assumed value in $).

Goals ⟶

Understanding application efficiencies	Process handover reduction	Being compliant	Assessing supply chain advantages	Designing the right business case	Creating data to support decision making
▣ ▢ ▢	▢ ▢	▣ ▢	▢ ▢		▣

A second stage in the development of this initiative will be to attach some of the work areas above onto a project wall that is structured around these goals (represented by the cards in the goals' table). But for now let's continue with the original goals we set ourselves.

GOAL 2: ACHIEVING SOME UPLIFT IN BRAND COMMUNICATIONS.

A similar breakdown can be made for brand communications. Brands get good value out of being perceived as innovators. Reputation can raise stock price and create a feel good factor internally and externally. Breaking that project down early on can show how you intend to use reputation as one significant strand of investment return.

GOAL 3: CRAFTING A BASE STATION DESIGN.

Now we are getting into the technical domain. What examples can we uncover of base station design and staffing? How will an insurance company manage base stations? Will it use a third party? How will it integrate base station communications into its own systems? Will base stations process the data from the drones? This starts to become a quite significant set of projects with an expanding range of business goals to help guide work breakdown.

Goals →

Understand applications	Be compliant	Assess supply chain factors	Have the right business case including brand uplift	Create data to support decision making	Optimise base station protocols	Identify launch partners in claims' processing

GOAL 4: DESIGNING COMMUNICATIONS PROTOCOLS.

Very relevant to goal 3, what will be the protocols that allow drones to communicate information that could be decisive in legally binding settlements? This is partly a technical question - what kinds of image compression, which networks, and partly a legal question: what constitutes proof when it is acquired by a robotics technology?

GOAL 5: CREATING EXPERTISE IN SECURITY ISSUES.

Finally this whole project will come to nothing if the security and overall integrity of the data is not as close to foolproof as possible. That means compliance with standards and so on.

When you begin to talk about those goals, how you see value will depend on the type of culture in your company. Google is seen as a data-driven company, for example. It likes to project that image. However, it is also extremely skilled at projecting the idea that it works on the edge of innovation. This reputation plays into its stock price, as well as supporting its global recruitment drive. There is huge value in building an innovation reputation. Maybe this is a place to begin work, at least for one part of the team. It can be assigned to social communications people who can begin to craft different ways the story of innovation can be leaked into the public domain. Work breakdown can now begin on that.

It could also be, though, that insufficient attention is being paid to the technical requirements of this initiative. If that is the case, and you are driven by technical skills or believe digital transformation is defined by technology, then you need to draft areas of work relative to those needs.

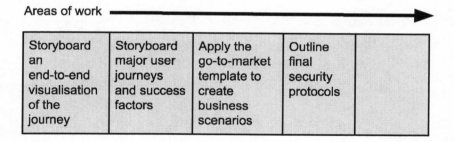

Storyboard an end-to-end visualisation of the journey	Storyboard major user journeys and success factors	Apply the go-to-market template to create business scenarios	Outline final security protocols	

You also begin to think about adapting your go-to-market (GTM) template. The consumer-goods company Procter and Gamble, in its heyday as an innovator, never gave a green light to projects without first applying their GTM template.

You have now reached the place where your priority areas of work are:

1.   Storyboarding the overall journey and experience.

2.   Getting perspectives on this.

3.   Working out the GTM and comms strategy

The first of these will lead you into technical requirements. The next two will never be complete until those requirements are well understood.

The team can now start to prioritise the goals, as areas of work become obvious and value becomes more visible.

The priority as Sean said, is to see where the value lies. Who gains from having a drone at a disaster site? What type of drone service would be needed in order for people to gain? And how can we begin to express that value through the work breakdown?

That might lead a team to prioritise understanding work at the site of an adverse weather event, how to direct cameras to capture significant images, what degree of AI processing would be needed to ensure image standardisation or disambiguation, how to protect the images from interference on site, how the images can best be streamed into the data centre, what types of compression and storage to use and so on, as well as how to interface with emergency services, which may or may not have arrived, and what degree of anonymity is prudent for people at the site. These areas of work allow you to understand how to prioritise goals.

What we say in Flow is that no single brain can figure all this out. And nobody can be sure of how to source all the facets of expertise needed to do good planning. What we do know is that if everybody is looking at the problem we stand a higher chance of:

- Covering off all the detail so we know that good work can flow through our processes.

- Identifying all the technical, legal and social dependencies.

- Understanding who can get value from this and when.

And a way to ensure cooperation among colleagues is to express the work not as an Epic but as a business goal or outcome that they codesign and manage flexibly over time.

If you don't have a business goal, you won't be thinking about value. You will be thinking about work. If you don't have a flexible business goal, it is very difficult to set the scene for cooperation between people from different backgrounds because there is no focal point for that cooperation. Too much is cut and dried. With flexible business goals at every level of a new initiative you have shared objectives that you can test together.

NEARLY THE END OF USER STORIES AND PERSONAS

User Stories are a formal technique in Agile. They are usually based on a Persona and of course Personas are widely used also in marketing. The formality of User Stories in Agile leads to some pretty dreary work experiences. Using this method developers or analysts have to state all the possible requirements that a system or feature has to perform for each persona. This leads to multiple repetitions of:

As a customer I want to …. In order that I can….

Stated at a high enough level these Stories or statements can inspire developers or marketers towards good work. Often though they become part of the overall Alcatraz of Agile. They become a prison that is tied back to a testing suite and a set of obligations to code work of dubious value.

So to find a way around this, back to Sean and work breakdown. The way that engineers have been used to working was for the business side of the house to push their requirements to the business analysts who would then document requirements for development teams to work on. In Agile these would then be stated as those As a customer... or as a Developer... routines.

And even in Agile there is a sense in which two sides, business and IT, have separate domains and don't really come together much.

The value of Flow lies partly in changing that. By maintaining flexible goals Flow creates interaction between the business and IT. Less work is imprisoned in requirements and those dreary "As a customer…." statements.

In particular the emphasis on a very short cycle-time ensures people quickly get evidence of what is working with users/customers; therefore where value lies and where, in contrast, energy is being squandered. These observations can set the conditions for much better interaction between different disciplines and hence lead to better decisions.

"The business was always tempted to stuff a document with everything they could think of because they never knew what the implications were, in terms of budget, timescales etc," says Sean. "Now the business specifies the goals and participates in defining and reviewing how goals are met. It can mean the business reordering their priorities on the fly as the development process shows us that some features are not going to work or some need prioritising.

We've also empowered developers to ask what is the business value of what I am producing whereas they used to be inclined to just get on with the work.

Because we break the work down as late as possible we can also bring the latest context to that.

Typically when we start out on a new project or goal our cycle-times are longer, like 2-3 weeks. But as delivery gains momentum we get that down. We're learning. That learning provides context for the next breakdown and it improves our dependencies' identification.

We also make sure we do at least one breakdown or review session a week where all the domain specific skills are in the room or at the wall.

We've learned not to do work breakdown in a technical language and technical steps. It's really about finding a way to capture user-journeys or work-flows and therefore break down the work into vertical slices of incremental deliverables.

You can use the Agile techniques like User Stories but we think of a story as anything we're being told by customers or anything that captures their needs, so the story can be a narrative, an example, or set of examples, a drawing or it can be a formal document, but it's whatever works.

By creating formal documents you tend to have people go away and do their interpretation of what was said and then a week or so later you're potentially stuck arguing over whether that's the right interpretation - maybe your interpretation is wrong! So it's about whatever technique you have that can immediately capture that sense of creating value, something we've had a conversation about and decided on."

This is a much less formal way of working but as more demanding one in that most of what happens is negotiated between smart people. It prioritises the instantaneous or real-time over planning and projects. It adapts the User Story idea and strips out the formality. User journeys can be captured any old way and neither developers nor business leaders need to be stuck with dozens of statements about what a customer might want to do - we accept what customers really want will emerge when they interact with us.

DESIGNING UNITS OF WORK IN HOLISTIC TEAMS

In Flow, we want to disrupt the User Story process, and the handover of requirements, by providing light frameworks for IT and business to codesign work. In this next example, rather than looking at the work design of a wholly new initiative, we have taken a small segment of a work-in-progress.

The scenario is one we have mentioned earlier. We are trying to design a survey that will give us deeper insights into why customers do not return for car servicing. We want those insights to lead to new customer relationship initiatives. As the survey will be online, this is a cooperation between IT and marketing.

Our habit as a car company is to look at what we want to get out of our distributor network, how many parts we can sell and how we can apply pressure on customers. But we want to turn that round. How can we help them more? In reality we have no idea what that question means. The reason is we are fixated on our need for continuous parts' sales not on their need for success. We have to start thinking outside of our own selfish culture so that we can understand what success feels like on the day our customers visit us for a service or repair.

How do *we* design new services or features that customers will discover and want to embrace? How do we get to that point quickly, and how can we test for value along the way?

In the table below we show a high level breakdown created for a holistic team (in the next chapter we will look at more detailed work breakdown). At this stage we are still trying to figure out our new way of thinking. In this work matrix we are, as always, pushing to the point where each work unit will be only two days long. First, we need a conversation about the major areas of work.

What is the statement of proposed value here? *We believe that by producing or changing x we can create measurably better outcomes for different classes of customers and reduce churn at our distributorships by y%.*

MULTIDISCIPLINARY WORK AREAS

Business goals	Understand variety of unmet needs in the market	Provide a framework for reconfiguring our approach to channels	Be hyper-relevant to customers	Plan for the whole lifecycle of customer experience	Create data to support decision making
Work Areas	1	2	3	4	5
Improving the customer journey	Create new customer segmentation analysis. Explore design-for-sharing issues.	Provide an end to end description of customer journey in each relevant segment.	Identify product discovery points - where customers will encounter or discover the new product.	Expand understanding of downstream costs and gains for customers.	Create list of customer success factors.
Areas of work	Socialise initial requirements. Analyse social media data. Create Customer Innovation Wall.	Explore existing assets suited to delivery into these segments; explore partner assets.	Define MSD Matrix (features to be exposed to customers first) where value will be tested.	Break work down into tasks that can be allocated to teams for further analysis.	Begin development of initial matrix.
Devise success and test criteria	Observe behaviours in customer lab. Specify usability features. Elicit success factors. Specify shareability options.	Define customer gains by segment. Experiment with internal users.	Define a flexible test plan. Create shared language and criteria of success for the work.	Create a cohort plan (how to migrate customers to better outcomes and less churn).	Agree just-in-time testing process.
Plan for content and marketing	Explore messaging options.	Describe where thought leadership opportunities exist. Identify social media options per channel.	Define website content including explainers. Plan to test. Design shareable content.	SEO optimise. Define customer self-service content. When to introduce A/B test?	Develop a traction plan to support uptake, and post-production engagement

This kind of process, going from goals to breakdown, restating the next level of goals and breaking work down further - is far better than business colleagues creating a specification that IT then describes in Epics and Stories. But think of this as just one iteration because in the next chapter we will address the same issues again at a different level of detail. Bear in mind too that there is no wrong way of doing this.

In this breakdown we are fleshing out an area of the Flow Value Stack by driving our work breakdown with a Go-To-Market Plan. The plan prioritises:

- A holistic understanding of the customer journey including downstream consequences.

- Designing for shareability.

- Testing in a just-in-time manner.

- Defining the value-gains.

We are avoiding older concepts like the business model canvas and the value proposition. What we're pursuing instead is a sense of what it takes to capture a customer's attention so that we can get them to test our concepts.

Below the business goals, the top row consists of a customer journey analysis and is driven by a Go-To-Market plan emphasising ways that customers discover a product or service and the journey customers take once the discovery is made. That first point is so vital to your design objectives. How do customers discover what you want them to embrace?

The second point is no less important. What will be their journey from where (prior to discovery) to later (some time after using the product or service, to the point of sharing and extending its value).

The second strand is: how might this begin to shape up as areas of work for developer teams. All of these elements will be further broken down into smaller units of work on a Kanban Wall but what can a holistic team already make of it?

Success factors make up strand 3. What makes the product easily usable? Shareable? And how can those ideas be tested along the way? This integrates with customer segment analysis and traction planning - user experience of a minimum sustainable delivery matrix feeds into this.

Critical to online projects is a sense of what types of content will support discovery, launch and traction, including customer self-service routines. Some kind of wireframe for content is necessary as much of it will live online.

We think these kinds of templates help people to get visual work off to a good start. It can be daunting to stand in front of colleagues and attempt to define a project off-the-bat in a visual way. A good way to start is to have a framework like this available but as always adapt and create your own.

CHAPTER 6

Creating Value-Seeking Behaviour

In the last Chapter we looked at work breakdown as a social art. In Chapter 6 we want to continue in that vein by asking: how do we seek value as a continuous activity without a spreadsheet, value proposition or a conventional ROI? How do we seek value as part of our regular conversations?

We have already drawn attention to the Flow Value Stack as a set of methods that generate value-seeking behaviour and in this chapter we will go into more detail on some of them.

The fundamental question - how do we seek value - is routinely overlooked when teams set up projects. There are techniques like Value Management and Value Stream Mapping, both of which we mentioned earlier. We agree with the Value Management philosophy of balancing costs and features but we believe we need to make value-seeking part of our everyday activities rather than a separate piece of analytical work. Formal techniques will slow work down. They are also hard to apply when units of work are down to two days. At that level of granularity, we want to be progressing through a quick test of value (such as a just-in-time acceptance test or an A/B test).

We also said earlier that value analysis is mostly subjective (up to the point where enough people buy a product or use a service).

We talk about value propositions, value management, value mapping, and product-market fit. They all sound like methodologies for ensuring value but in fact they are all subjective. Let's embrace subjectivity and make it part of our peer conversation. Talking in a critical way helps create some objectivity.

Often we are doing work where little thought was given to how a project will unfold in a value-driven way. Leaders assume a project has value because of the ROI estimates. That's why it has been given the green light. The main task is to complete it.

This tendency to build belief in an idea or project before work has begun, will not go away. But what if the project soon looks like a dud? Or what if many of the components of a project block value rather than add to it?

We talk about value-seeking as an everyday behaviour in order to answer those questions. Actually we do it so that we can ask those questions much more often. We don't want to do work that has no value or chase a project to an unsatisfactory end. We want to be asking value-questions about many aspects of the work.

We'll use a couple of examples here from the first Flow book to see how we go about doing that. In the process we are seeking 80% of the value from 20% of the resources while discarding unvaluable work. We began this process in Chapter 2 with CATE. In the previous chapters we have also looked at work breakdown and visualisation as ways to uncover value. We are on our way to value-seeking behaviour.

SOME VALUE STORIES

In the 1970s and 1980s the United States' television receiver industry came under sustained attack from Japanese manufacturers (just to be clear the "receiver" is the TV set).

American companies like RCA had built substantial integrated businesses on the back of black and white TV receiver manufacture, content production, broadcasting and advertising. In the meantime, in the background, they pioneered the mass production of colour TVs. All these businesses went bust! By the 1990s the original American TV companies had lost out to Sony and co. Later, the Japanese lost out to the Koreans.

What was the secret of Japanese success? The answer is two-fold: continuous improvement and taking a holistic market view rather than focusing only on innovation. These two aspects should alert everyone to what happens with innovation. You can be really smart about tech products but you cannot divorce that from how you view customers and their segmentation.

In this 1970s, US companies introduced a lot of semiconductor technology to the TV set in order to outsmart the Japanese. However it turned out that the Japanese were better than US companies at optimising semiconductor manufacture. Semiconductor manufacture has a steep learning curve and the Japanese did ***continuous learning*** much more consistently than the Americans, who were far better at innovation.

But second, there was a different kind of perspective on how markets function. US companies drove towards excellence, producing TV sets of the highest possible image quality. The Japanese optimised rather than maximised.

US-made TV sets had a high rate of valve burnout caused by the demands of superior images. That meant customers of US sets had to call for the repair-engineer regularly. The Japanese had optimised to ensure less valve burnouts and less repairs. They under-innovated the image and had less need of field repair teams.

A similar example can be seen at Netflix. Netflix supplies servers to cable head-ends to store content ready for local distribution.

It optimised the design of these servers to make them especially rugged. They are more expensive than normal servers but they have both a longer lifespan and less need of repair. In fact, Netflix does not repair them. If they develop faults they are replaced. Costly, you might think, but the company has avoided the huge ongoing expense of a field engineering workforce, saving a fortune in overhead and disgruntled partners.

These are examples of looking for value across a matrix of activity rather than driving for efficiency in any single, or discrete, area. They are also beautifully simple ideas that have helped create world class companies. In Flow we similarly need to look for how a matrix of activity is best optimised.

FLOW VALUE OPTIMISATION ANALYSIS

In the bulk of this chapter we will be looking at value-seeking behaviour but we want to start by looking at the longer term. Periodically we need to review our processes and test for value. How do we go about doing that? We'll dig a little deeper here.

In the world of manufacturing engineers talk about value-stream analysis. This concept has been transferred over to software production. By extension it means that any project of a digital nature probably undergoes a value-stream analysis somewhere.

Value stream analysis is a highly detailed review of all work processes and its purpose is for engineers to take out waste.

Despite its name it is rare to use such an analysis to ask: Are we actually creating value here? Or, more to the point, are we optimising the way we create value? In many engineering environments taking out waste is equivalent to creating more value. Value=waste reduction.

In Flow, we have begun to talk about Value Optimisation Analysis (or Reviews) in place of value-stream analysis, in order to raise questions about our processes. A Flow Value Optimisation Analysis is a periodic sanity check on the work we are doing. It has that Value Stream element - can we get rid of waste? But it has a big difference too.

In Flow Value Optimisation we are asking people to keep an open and curious mind in order to address the bigger question: Does what we are doing make good sense, in that it creates value and does so in a balanced way?

Earlier we spoke about this in terms of all the different activities a company now has to manage. In the midst of all this can we say that we are optimising our investments (in people, ideas, processes) in such a way that customers or internal users benefit?

In most businesses a process to analyse a question like this would have a formal *scorecard*. It would be implemented at regular intervals. It would be standardised and there would be a report produced from it. By the time the report is actioned, life will have moved on. In place of these rigid structures, how about we trust people to have a regular conversation about value.

There are some more useful tools to feed into this that we will look in Chapter 10:

- The Customer Feedback Wall - a critical element of the Flow Value Stack.

- Predictive metrics such as inbound inquiries, one of many new metrics suggested by the SaaS community.

These tools provide invaluable insight for Flow Value Optimisation analysis. They all help pose questions about value. The issues we want to discuss can be reflected on a Flow Value Wall with the usual Post-Its recording answers in tweet length messages. First though what are the issues?

A value review or analysis starts with a timeblock, say, a three month period. As with all issues in the modern workplace you do not want to overload each other. Coming away with three points to improve on is good. These are the types of questions that can guide you.

1. What have been our big successes in terms of customer uptake over the past three months?

2. Have we been meeting our 1 - 2 day cycle-time objective so that we can pivot easily and reduce code collisions; if not where are the blockers?

3. How many customer feedback issues have been dealt with and how can we classify these?

4. What trends can we observe on the Customer Feedback Wall that reveal some consistent problems with how features get passed through to customers?

5. How many of these issues are strategic and what do we think this says about our larger, strategic goals and our understanding of customers?

6. How many features are under-used and adding cost without delivering value?

7. Are enough of our products and features contributing to customer success?

8. In that context, how are our customers' journeys changing? Are we holistic enough in how we understand their overall experience?

9. What is the story of those features? What has been their life-cycle with us? When were they introduced and why? Is there anything in our processes that can explain why we missed the pivot?

10.   What key lessons have been captured on the Learning Wall?

11.   Are the ideas on the Cool Wall creating clear value when they are implemented as new tools? Is any feedback problem associated with the introduction of new tools?

12.   Are we suffering from inadequate dependency analysis and why is the Risks and Issues Wall not performing for us?

13.   Can we identify any consistent blockers that should force us to address a process or staffing issue?

14.   What is our current trend of inbound inquiry and which types of content are working best for us?

15.   Is the review signalling any new key competency needs?

16.   How are we as a group feeling about our performance? Is there a sense of excitement that we have things to learn here, are there lessons for personal development goals (see Chapter 11) or is any part of our process design feeling like a burden?

These are conversations between smart people rather than reports from experts. They have to be reviewed informally because once you turn this into a significant reporting mechanism you will fire up a blame game.

In place of that, think instead of smart folks taking on the responsibility of revising their work practices because they want to. They want to ask these questions because it leads them closer to their behavioural goal of seeking value rather than just doing work.

The discussion can be summarised on a Flow Value Wall as below. Additional columns could be added that give more detail about the action implied by any successes, gains or added value. Trends, however, can teach us more. Maybe the trend is negative, in the sense that in certain areas we are losing value.

Flow Optimisation Analysis

	Customer Feedback	Work design	Tools deployed	Features	Learning and capabilities
Trends	▢	▢	▢	▢	
Wins		▢	▢	▢	
Value	$$	$$$			$$
Actions					

In this Wall you can see along the top the facets of work that you want to assess. You could adapt it to marketing by adding in Social Media Activities or to logistics with a column for, say, Automation Activities.

The idea is to take a view on the trends you are seeing (use a yellow Post-It for negative and a blue one for positive). Where you have clear wins. What these gains are in $ (small, medium or large; $, $$, $$$); and what actions your analysis suggests.

The optimisation assesses the value-logic of processes, features and functions that have been in place for a while. But first we need to learn how to optimise value day-to-day. That's what we'll concentrate on now.

VALUE PROPOSITIONS AND VALUE SEEKING BEHAVIOUR

Very often in business the idea of value is framed as a ***value proposition***. Value propositions are another example of business literature being dominated by the needs of startups or new products. Bear in mind we are seeking something different: How to maintain a continuous flow of innovations that we can test with customers.

The usual way to define a value proposition reflects the fact that startups don't have customers. Here is a couple to chew on, one from Forbes:

In its simplest terms, a value proposition is a positioning statement that explains what benefit you provide for who and how you do it uniquely well. It describes your target buyer, the problem you solve, and why you're distinctly better than the alternatives.

And one from the dictionary:

an innovation, service, or feature intended to make a company or product attractive to customers

We think of a value proposition as something much more complex and encompassing. You can see from the examples we gave of Japanese TV manufacture and Netflix servers that the value proposition is also the search for value through the optimisation of resources across the whole customer experience. It cannot be encapsulated in one sentence nor in one project. Nor does it ever end. Like all things modern in business it is open ended and continuous.

The idea of a value proposition being a singular statement of value and uniqueness is quite different from the position many, if not most, large companies find themselves in.

In established enterprises the search for value arises in two main ways.

1. How can I be sure that my work-in-progress and projected investments are adding value to customers in a balanced or optimised way? That can also be framed as: How can I be sure my activity and investments are helping my customers to succeed with their lives and that this is sustainable (economically, for us, environmentally, for the world, and morally, for society)?

2.   What initiatives can we develop to expand our markets as new technologies arise and new needs become evident?

We'll leave position 2 alone for now and focus on position 1. The key question is:

I have a substantial amount of work-in-progress, and more in the backlog, more still in the Portfolio plan, so how do I assure myself that each work unit we embark on is helping customers to get what they want or need, especially as I transition to new ways of work (the Flow Value Optimisation Analysis would ask that retrospectively)?

SEEKING VALUE WITHOUT WRITING VALUE PROPOSITIONS

The normal way that companies go about creating value is project-based. We've already argued against this.

The reason is simply that projects have a beginning, middle and end with a number of reporting obligations imposed on milestones. They are so formalised and over-burdened by management tools that they have become the wrong units of work for the modern enterprise. Projects typically fail or disappoint because they provide an inappropriate management framework for innovation, certainly in today's climate.

Many companies are not only inventing a new product or two: they are responding to system changes. Those changes might be: the introduction of drones, autonomous cars and the rearchitecting of the global transport infrastructure, the Internet of Things, digital currencies.

In all these cases, the enterprise has to invent a way to deal with reality. The "project" is out there, in the ecosystem. It is being done to you and your environment.

Dealing with this through the old project approach would just take too long. The answer is to identify what your goals are in the sphere of the IoT or drones or autonomous cars. As you begin to break work down, the granularity of goals becomes more detailed. However, it is still the goals that matter (you might want to refer back to Chapter 5 for an earlier iteration of this process).

Goals drive a continuous flow of activity in units of work that are overseen or managed by being visible and open to the scrutiny of peers. The work design relies on the social interaction between smart people and the application of their collective intelligence.

ANOTHER PARTIAL VIEW OF THE FLOW VALUE STACK

Work Breakdown 1: The statement of proposed value: make value statements about the opportunity, the technology, the markets and the business objectives, expressed in $ where possible. And the proposed value to users.

Work breakdown 2: Articulate the goals. Set out the business objectives in detail, bringing in domain experts to propose chunks of work that would deliver the objectives, prioritising the objectives that would deliver value fastest; refer back to segments.

Work breakdown 3: Capturing user success factors. Articulate the needs of users within a system. Identify features that clearly bring greater success earlier. Expose dependencies between chunks of work and architecture. Iterate with goals to accelerate value.

Work breakdown 4: Create areas and units of work. Iteratively break the work down going from goals to large areas of work to small units of work achievable in 2 days. Apply a go-to-market model as far as possible to keep customers front of mind. Iterate with step 3.

Work breakdown 5: Deliver test and iterate. Informally test all work for value. Argue with the business goals as work continues. Question data and assumptions. Tie work to customer feedback loops that feed into Kanban Walls and Portfolio planning. Do J-i-T tests in informal groups.

We avoid the idea that any of the units of work that follow from this are projects that have a separate life from the search for value. So the question we asked in the book Flow was how do you take business objectives and work them into value?

There are a few formal methodologies for doing this such as the Google Design Print or the McKinsey Concept Sprint. Both involve 5 day cycles of ideation and prototyping. These are good methods but what we are about to describe is something that emerges from practice rather than something that is a designed method. By all means use the Google Design Sprint or incorporate it into the Flow Value Stack.

Like work breakdown, the process of innovating in a multi-tiered matrix is partly an art. But the idea of value brings discipline to what you are doing. The sheer volume of innovation requires you to adopt value-seeking behaviour in order to make good decisions. Increasingly we are faced with system-wide change rather than simply evolving a new product and our observations are based on that broader need.

Here are two examples.

EXAMPLE 1: CHANGING THE BUSINESS CYCLE IN INSURANCE

Because large firms have multiple systems in place, there is often a system-cycle that goes with innovation. Think of this as a phase-change issue. In phase changes a substance can go from a solid to a liquid to a gas. It is the same substance differently expressed.

Certain types of innovations have a system-wide impact that resembles a phase change. Imagine electric vehicles and the impact they are having on the system of distributing gasoline and electricity. Imagine the hydrogen car and what that will do to the system supporting transportation.

Systems protect incumbents, like oil producers, but there are times when the roots of innovation are so obvious and the need so great that the system becomes surprisingly malleable. Change begins to happen without anybody writing a value proposition. It becomes our job to catch up as systems begin to disintegrate or morph.

Another example is the blockchain. It is changing how we view currencies and accounting, two fundamentals of the economy. Nobody wrote the blockchain value proposition or the Bitcoin MVP. It will radically alter supply chain management without anybody going near a business model canvas. These are artefacts imposed on the startup world but they are not necessary when systems begin to disintegrate and reform.

That's what's happening with drones in insurance. In Flow, we touched on the likely future use of drones to help collect information about traffic accidents and in the process add value by being an independent observer of events following an accident.

However, drones have become quickly adapted by insurance companies in part because of the increase in adverse weather events. They have introduced a phase change in the way insurance functions.

Insurers have always been set up to deal with a periodic catastrophe but such events are now increasing in frequency. Frequency places claims and settlement systems under unbearable strain. As one insurance executives said to us: We are set up to deal with one catastrophe but those events are multiplying and we cannot cope.

Drones can help resolve that crisis. They are now providing data for better underwriting of risk; assessing claims after an event;

speeding up the payment of claims; and accelerating the process of compiling claims for the ultimate underwriter, the Lloyd's Syndicate.

The development of drones in this application area has been rapid, beginning in 2014. It is difficult to portray this development as a minimum viable product that built iteratively towards a new product that a company put on the market.

Reaping the benefits of drones is the key question. Catching up is the task. Improvements in drone software continue to hone the performance for this application; improvements in data integration and software will continue to improve claims processing for years to come; and adverse events will benefit from faster adjuster cycle-time. The issue is not how to write the MVP but how to get to highest value fastest and most prudently. And that is happening in the new normal way. Value formation arises from a vast matrix of activities.

Insurers are working with small expert firms in the field of drone applications to iterate and build the experience of dealing with quicker and better data. They need to know how that can be integrated into insurer processes (or how those processes need to change). They need to figure out how to develop and manage a drone fleet, what compliance issues arise, where and when to deploy, and how to adopt machine learning to help deal with the scale of data that drones will create.

Each of these would become a matrix of mini-two-day units of work in Flow.

In short though, this is not a product development cycle. It is a phase change-cycle that has multiple strands and layers of innovation that need to take place simultaneously. Within all this the constant question will be to discover where the best value lies.

EXAMPLE 2: CREATING VALUE IN TRANSPORT

Here's a second example. In the car industry much of the R&D, marketing and advertising goes into selling cars, usually through distributors. However, much of the profit comes from selling parts.

We pointed out in Chapter 2 that the car industry is tolerably good at customer segmentation for sales. Curiously it is the luxury car makers (most obviously BMW and Mercedes) that are particularly good at segmentation. However, few car makers are good at segmenting their After-Sales customers. You may remember we raised this problem again, briefly, in Chapter 4, where we had a first iteration at breaking down work for an online survey and we looked at it again in Chapter 5. We will now go into that overall problem in more detail.

To summarise:

- Many enterprises do not have problems that can be solved with a startup approach such as MVP.

- They struggle to balance complex psychological and financial pressures.

- After-Sales is where the profit lies.

- Car makers have little idea how this market segments other than data on the types of cars that get serviced most.

- Car makers think they can solve this problem with a big data solution, or "markets of one."

PHASE 1. THE STATEMENT OF PROPOSED VALUE

We articulate a set of general statements about the market segments, the problems, the technology, the options, success factors and so on with an emphasis on the value we will bring to customers. The $ value could come under the business goals (phase 2)

By looking at the customer segmentation we can see new opportunities. Let's just focus on one.

As we pointed out in Chapter 2, females disproportionately follow After-Sales on social media. There is something in here that hints at a possibility for more customer success. Is there an opportunity to enhance some segment of the female experience of After-Sales support, attract word-of-mouth marketing for our services, increase the customer retention after the warranty period, raise parts and service revenues and through this positive experience create more excitement around the brand?

As well as these valuable sentiments, we need a $ value for this opportunity. And it could be our goal is to increase female retention rates by 10% overall and understand female success factors across each segment of the market. That might give us an overall 1 or 2% lift in sales value.

We could also set other valuable outcomes. As the car industry grows more towards a platform business we could argue that we need experience of developing new partnerships and ecosystems. Who else could provide solutions for us in the area of female customer success factors?

PHASE 2: ARTICULATING FLEXIBLE BUSINESS GOALS

The main business goal is to bring customers back to service garages well beyond the point where their warranty expires. This seems to conflict with the success factors that shape customer behaviour (as most mass market car buyers do not return).

Distributor servicing is often more expensive than the neighbourhood garage; the experience of handing the car over is often rushed and sometimes aggressive. Distributorships are often on the edge of town, which provides conveniently cheap retail space but it means customers struggle to organise transport into work or back to the garage to pick up the car.

On the other hand the neighbourhood garage offers very few guarantees.

Traditionally this problem has been dealt with by imploring the customer to use genuine parts, with the implicit warning that non-genuine parts are dangerously inferior. Even so customers refuse to make the trip back.

Should the car maker switch out of threat mode and create better experiences of distributorships? At least it can go into the hypotheses. We might be able to find a better context for distributor garage experiences.

Big data could also be a help. The idea of a big data project in this situation is to find out what co-factors appear when analysing people returning to garages. There is an expectation that these will reveal success factors that can be spread around to other customers. An AI can go further and help identify events that lead to purchases and can be used to trigger the visit through replicating some aspects of other user journeys. But any company wanting to implement an AI will wait a long time to see success. We are after the short term.

If we settle back and start to articulate the business goals they should be something like:

- To find ways to enhance customer success in different segments.

- To understand those segments better.

- To bring happy customers back to the distributor service centre in a positive context, through more tailored experiences.

- To build new partnerships where these can add value.

As always these become part of a visual interaction between people and between goals and tasks.

Major goals

Make a difference	Enhance segmentation	Improve retention by a defined amount	Extend partnering capability

Outside the world of formal project management, no goal is ever static. More goals will emerge as we break the work down. We are prepared also to see the goals change as we understand more (or use a slightly different approach as in Chapter 5). Bear in mind also that this opportunity sits along many others we're working on. So point 1 is we are articulating goals but we are also going to learn how to be flexible with them and to manage that flexibility up and down the hierarchy.

PHASE 3: UNDERSTANDING CUSTOMER SUCCESS FACTORS

In this case we want to find ways to encourage women to experience car servicing in the most positive way possible. One way into this kind of problem used to be the user survey or focus group. For a period during the 1970s - 2000s these were accompanied by other techniques such as ethnography. These techniques have fallen out of favour as technologists have promised more value through data analytics.

Nonetheless, we still believe in them. They can be added into a project that also uses call-centre analytics and social media sentiment analysis to provide a comprehensive picture of customer pain points. The question we want to answer is what makes customers' lives tangibly better; so much better that they will pay a premium to keep this experience in their lives and potentially share it with friends and family?

For this part of the program, we might bring in sociologists and/ or psychologists to help us understand what success factors look like for different segments of the female After-Sales market. However, there is one change from the past. These experts will have to take an experimental approach to their work. What we want from them is the opportunity to set up experiments that we can test and iterate.

It's a fair bet that with the emphasis on female customers some aspect of the solution will involve relationships. Distributorships can be confrontational and manipulative and, while these sales techniques worked in the past, we have to test whether they have run their course.

The questions we begin to ask therefore concern the culture of distributor garages, as well as transport to and from distributorships bearing in mind the propositions that:

a.   More women favour After-Sales than favour buying;

b.   Women are much more important in decision making than men are.

It's clear that several units of work can be built out of observing behaviour at garages. The very process of understanding customer success factors can become a good Flow project. What units of work would lead to improved understanding of female experiences?

We could use closed circuit TV or paid observers to do systematic observations at garages, on top of the data collection from call centres. But we want to articulate the work so that we are getting results after two days and not two months.

Our research experts pitch up at the Wall to exchange ideas on how best to glean insights without a huge amount of wait-time.

1.   Do we want some kind of travel diary for people attending garages - how far have they come, what means of transport, at what cost or degree of difficulty?

2.   Part of the task is to dive into market segmentation. Do we want to segregate this into male/female and into work

types (manual, office, executive or some other segmentation) as we dive into customer segments. Or do the social media insights offer a better route?

3.   Another source of value might be to observe interaction at a cross section of garages.

4.   We want to do some exit polling, i.e. asking customers what could have been better as they pick their cars up.

5.   Another goal though is to look to the future. We want to throw a curveball in there - what do younger people think of this environment, the next generation of car buyers, or will they mostly be car sharers and if so what does that mean for distributor real estate?

6.   We want to understand what different solutions might come out of this, and we can do a lot of anticipating before we get the results. For example, do we need to provide better online information about a car's life cycle value or personal safety? Would a mobility website help and if so how?

7.   A key business goal is to get users to become advocates. We need to answer the question: How would success play out on social media such that customers share out offers, values, ideas?

8.   As another goal is to increase our capacity to develop partnerships, there may be new product opportunities or alliances with apps like MyTaxi (offering discounts from the garage?) or at least looking at the coverage of car ride apps around distributorships so that we can theorise new ways to help people into work or to get home conveniently.

9.   We want to integrate with existing data sources. We need to tie the research into the insights we have from our on-board car apps in order to scale any benefits quickly.

10. We really want distributor staff to be more alert to different customer success factors. There could be additional online training modules needed for distributor staff that we should be thinking about.

11. We want to drive our go-to-market model right to the heart of the project. That means designing each component as an opportunity for customers to advocate and share good experiences, which in turn has to feed into every aspect of the experience we want to design.

12. We start to speculate about some form of gamification where customers earn points or some other reward based on their interaction with us. Maybe this is the answer to the survey problem. A suggestion goes up on the Wall to have a Twitter campaign offering $25 off a service in return for completing a survey within the next 48 hours. Currently we see them once every six months but a more continuous relationship will allow us into a relationship where they earn better pricing and now we have a reason to get out there on social media to connect with them as codesigners of a new level of service.

13. We need a way to monitor the value creation both from a customer's perspective and our own - are we headed to our 10% improvement target and how can we be sure?

14. We want to be a little bit left field. Assume cost is a big issue for female customers, are there new forms of pay-

ment that the garages should experiment with? Can we learn from Amazon Prime?

15.   We want everything to scale. What opportunities exist for collecting new data to help scale solutions up?

16.   And we need to understand impacts. There will be implications for software architecture.

All of this is taking place on a public Wall so that we can start to see units of work evolving. But the goals have already changed.

Major goals

Make a difference	Enhance segmentation	Improve retention	Extend partnering capability	Create market roadmap	Create advocates

In fact the goals will extend even further as we begin to work on the detail (see the next table below). In Agile, all this might be called writing the Epic on the way to writing the User Stories. The use of goals, though, forces us to keep orienting towards value.

Major goals ⟶

Make a difference	Enhance segmentation	Improve retention	Extend partnering capability	Create market roadmap	Create advocates	Optimise value
Survey output should identify customer success factors	Analytical work to better target innovation	Implement measures for specific segments	Identify ecosystem to add value to customers	Create an inter-generational perspective	Explore content options and social media options to propagate success factors	Sketch and analyse the variety of user perspectives

The breakdown is now giving us some major task areas. That one on the right, we will come to it later. Clearly the most important of these is to understand what success looks like to customers and in order to do that we need to work simultaneously on the market segmentation.

We also have to ask how can we understand the overall work activity from different perspectives? What for example would be the success factors for distributors or garage managers?

The customer is one user but the system includes distributors, garage managers, mechanics, payment systems, taxis. Though we can't spell all this out right now we do have an opportunity to ask which of these activities gives us the shortest route to value (for customers)?

What would tangibly add value to the outcomes they want to achieve? From a car driver perspective: Is it savings on a car service, improving residual values of the car, just getting to the garage more easily or cheaply, is it flexibility in scheduling, being less confronted by gender insensitivity, or what other success factors do they have?

From a distributor service manager's perspective: Is it to be sure of maximising service throughput each day; is each day already maximised, is there an optimal alternative to maximisation (for example is the imperative to maximise throughout each day coming at the cost of upsetting customers who then don't return), is there anything on the cost of customer acquisition that we can learn about that would help persuade distributorships to optimise rather than maximise?

From our own perspective: is it to minimise architectural impacts while meeting those business goals?

These questions need to be integrated as units of work under a separate goal: optimise value across the ecosystem.

In normal project planning we would already have progressed to the schedule of activities according to a production sequence drawn from the world of manufacturing - what has to be done first and what follows on in sequence from that (that's how we go to PERT and GANTT charts).

As you can see in Flow we are still asking questions and allowing ourselves to be curious about options. We want to focus on where we can clearly gain value.

As the tasks and questions see more light the process creates a mini-inflection point for the business goals. We run into the inevitable questions about how sound those business objectives really are. And where are the clear priorities, based on our desire for maximising value early?

If a business goal looks like it is going to take a long time to achieve, we need to get a sense of its value and whether it is worth the wait. We need to consider adapting it if value is too far down the track.

PHASE 4. CREATING NEW UNITS OF WORK

In Step 4 we are looking at creating units of work that can be handed over for research, marketing and production.

The truth is, many organisations lack the degree of integration between these teams that would give you a rich work breakdown where marketing, business delivery and IT tasks appear on the same Walls.

In an IT environment the objective is to get your work breakdown to the point of simple statements of a user's needs. In a broader and more multidisciplinary project we have more scope to seek out value. Intuitively we might believe it lies in how servicing is paid for or how people arrange transport to and from the garage. We can start breaking those down into units of work.

This will be a series of cards with short statements on. In an IT environment these are very short agile-like user stories such as:

As a customer I want to be able to log-on so that I can initiate a session.

Or

As a customer I want to be able to watch a video on the page so that I don't have to be directed elsewhere.

In the broader environment we need to articulate a wider variety of tasks that include other functions such as marketing and finance. However, we can still break them down to something that reveals if work has value or not.

As the work starts to get broken down it becomes clear that there are more development options than we could see at the higher level of breakdown. We can also see that by breaking work down further we can add in tasks that allow us to understand value better.

In creating this short list we have gone back and fore adding tasks, seeing if they contribute to the mix, crossing tasks out, raising new questions and so on.

What comes out of this is a new level of transparency. This is a pre-Team Kanban breakdown where we are not looking to allocate tasks. We are aiming to understand how to get to the right tasks by developing on from the goals we stated earlier.

By forcing work out into the open we can truly understand what we are doing. We know what each of us has to take on and nobody can disappear for a fortnight on a project that adds no value. Here are some higher level work units, developing on from the first iteration of this work sequence provided in Chapter 4.

1. As a Flow value manager I need to devise a class of questions that the research will answer so that we can be more responsive to customer segments.

    a. From the perspective of a distributor what are the benefits of current servicing scheduling arrangements?

    b. From the perspective of the customer: What are the issues relating to comfort in dealing with distributorships?

    c. And what are the issues relating to timing and scheduling?

    d.   From the perspective of developers what are the major task areas?

    e.   From the perspective of the system owner what system architecture implications arise as a result of changes to a process?

2.   As the Flow value manager I also want to organise consensus on the desired outcomes of an online survey and a narrative survey at locations.

3.   I also need a draft list of questions to ask service customers in an online survey.

    a.   I need to devise categories for the questions and describe potential outcomes that the answers will yield.

    b.   I need to organise a standup to socialise the draft.

4.   As an analyst I need to

    a.   Choose a survey tool.

    b.   Convert the draft questions into an online survey.

    c.   Pilot the survey.

    d.   Research previous experience of the use of these tools for surveys.

5.   As a Flow value manager I need an evaluation of instant communications for the survey: Twitter, WhatsApp etc and any previous instances of their use for surveys.

6.   As a developer I need to create a graphical account of the customers' journey through the survey.

    a.   A customer will need an incentive to go to a landing page.

    b.   She will need to discover the opportunity.

c.   And she will arrive at a landing page that needs to communicate a powerful message to incite action.

d.   She will want a reward for completing a survey.

e.   She may wish to see a progress bar as she is completing a survey.

f.   Her journey will not end with the last question. At the least, she will want a thank you note but what if she also went into a draw for a prize or were given interesting snippets of information as the survey attracted more people?

g.   She will have a journey beyond the survey as she is drawn closer to the community we are creating.

7.   As an analyst I need a choice of survey databases

a.   I may need to agree criteria for the choice.

b.   I need a method for automating the analytics.

c.   I need a design for feeding data into a survey database.

d.   I may also face some compliance issues in some jurisdictions as I am collecting personal data.

8.   As a team we need to review the survey questions and the logic of the analytics.

9.   As a marketer I need a draft narrative survey for interaction with customers at concessions.

a.   I want to attend a nearby distributor and talk with five customers arriving for servicing to test the narrative survey.

    b.   I want to co-decide any incentives provided to get people to a landing page.

    c.   I want to design a gamified approach to survey completion.

10.   As a developer I need to:

    a.   Describe a self-service scheduling app for distributorships.

    b.   Evaluate existing self-service scheduling apps.

11.   As an analyst I need to evaluate: from the perspective of a taxi app-platform what would be the benefits of allowing us a brand opportunity on their app?

You can see some clear tasks being described here and yet there are also questions that need breaking down further so that they can be framed as two-day tasks. That process is iterative. If a task is on a wall somebody might already know the answer, say, to the right analytics for this survey so solutions can come faster than two days.

The point of Flow at this stage is to keep figuring out the smallest unit of work in relation to the goals. When you know those, you know more about resource allocation and estimating.

At the same time we can create second order goals. As we touched on it earlier, a clear example of this would be why we want to understand the distributor's perspective. Any implementation will have to win favour with that user group.

Part of the activity turns to understanding and articulating dependencies between the units of work and any risks and issues that might arise. But we don't try to anticipate all of this. Instead we use a Risks and Issues Wall to create a venue where risks and issues can be kept under continuous review.

PHASE 5. DELIVER, TEST AND ITERATE.

In Flow the test and iteration of ideas is continuous. We want the units of work under point 4 to deliver pilots or minimum sustainable delivery matrices that we can push to users/customers. But even some of the ideas about how we do our research need to be tested. We can test very informally. A test can simply be getting the right two or three people together and asking: Is this what we intended? Does it look like it has enough value?

In Agile there is a debate about the point at which work can actually be considered *done*. There is even a concept called *done, done*! That might mean that work has passed a series of acceptance tests and is definitively finished. In old software, big testing suites are designed at the start of projects. They soon become irrelevant and, in any case, few projects passed their tests. However, if one of these tests was an acceptance test and software got through, it would be considered *done, done*.

In the modern workplace, however, that point is rarely reached. Work is never really done because features are open to continuous improvement, especially as they are placed before users and as users gain experience of using them and their needs then adapt. So it is worth saying that the deliver, test and iterate cycle is not an end-point.

Deliver, test and iterate, also has a larger context of dealing with many new phenomena. We not only need to understand user-responses, we need to test and improve our own design skills, our strategic grasp of what's possible, and our understanding of the phase change. All that takes place with many statements about value but not a value proposition.

In Flow, then, we think of value-seeking rather than value propositions. We seek value in a number of ways:

1. In a Statement of Proposed Value we can hypothesise what we think will create value, assuming we can deliver on the promises of our projects.

2. By creating flexible business goals that people are equipped to adapt with on the spot decisions.

3. In breaking work down into tasks where value can more easily be identified and where we can dump what does not have value. These short cycles of work also reduce the potential for wasteful code collisions and context switching.

4. By engineering projects so that feedback loops are constantly creating information for strategists and KanBan teams

5. By conducting Flow Value Optimisation Analyses to check whether the systems, routines or services we've created continue to add value.

6. By engaging directly with the phase change and helping people to broaden their skills so they can put value ahead of roles.

7. We address value issues also through the Executive Portfolio Wall, a method for making sure, that only work of value passes down to the execution teams.

You can argue that the value proposition remains more important than these activities because it tries to tie your offer to a customer need. That's misleading, however.

Every time you ask questions about value you are seeking to provide more value to customers, either in the way you work, or the speed of adaptability or responsiveness. Being a company that relentlessly seeks value for customers is a highly impressive credential.

CHAPTER 7

The Agile C-Suite

There's a lot people can do to promote a more agile way of working and we've already touched on a few ideas in the previous 6 steps. However, the big issue for many people is rarely spoken out loud. Are executives making the right decisions? Are they making decisions that flow down to us as work of value or are we doing work we know to be a waste of time? You feel it in your bones. You know you are wasting your time but you have to appear "aligned".

In many respects value starts at the top and yet "the top" is often unaccountable for many decisions that don't optimise value. "The top" is responsible for making decisions that either create waste or let waste continue. These decisions filter down through the organisation and often get left there as zombie projects, months or years after their relevance passed away.

A recent Deloitte study, by the way, showed that a lack of executive accountability was one of the big corporate risk factors. That Deloitte report documents risks that can sink enterprises yet, at the same time, can be controlled if everybody takes their responsibilities seriously. Executive accountability, it concluded, is a big problem.

THE FOUR AWFUL CONSEQUENCES OF BAD EXECUTIVE DECISIONS?

1. Wasted resources.

2. More pressure on people to perform under constraint because resources are being wasted.

3. People disengaging because they know their work has no value.

4. Trouble innovating because there are too few resources and a feeling that we've tried new things in the past and they never went anywhere.

CREATING THE AGILE EXECUTIVE PORTFOLIO WITH FLOW

The way round this problem is to be very public about executive resource allocation. To challenge executives to be accountable is not easy. That's why we say executives have to lead the change. If they are not prepared to show how to change, fat chance for the rest of us.

One way to show a willingness is to create an Executive Portfolio Wall (EPW). The EPW becomes a public account of executive decision-making.

THREE AMAZING BENEFITS OF AN EPW:

1. Executives get to see how much resource they are wasting and then to put it right!

2. They get to see imbalances in resource allocation and are able to course-correct the organisation, ensuring that units of work are aimed at the right goals.

3.   They get to see emerging areas of activity that aren't cov-
      ered by their goals, areas that the mavericks have intro-
      duced in an attempt to create change - this is gold dust.

UNFREEZING MIDDLE MANAGEMENT

How do Executive Portfolio Wall's work? We devote a whole chapter to that in Flow. Fin has also written about it elsewhere, in particular on the need to create EPWs that provide oversight of executive impacts on IT, so let's try to combine the two.

In Flow implementations the chances are you will begin the whole Flow process with an EPW. They are that important; that pivotal. Creating a Wall with all the resources mapped against goals is not just a way to check if those resources are properly allocated. It is the beginning of a new dialogue between the most senior management and people who take responsibility for execution. The four or five major goals that guide an organisation have to be transplanted into operational goals by the CMO, CIO, CFO and so on. Team leaders in middle management, the ones most frozen out by change, get the opportunity to see these goals and to understand their changing roles, rather than just have change foisted upon them. The EPW becomes the fountainhead that starts the Flow. From here initiatives flow onto project walls and Kanban walls. The logic of the organisation and what it is trying to achieve is out there, on Walls being discussed.

So let's say the EPW is your start point and one of your aims is to make the continuity between executive decisions and middle management tasks visible.

Here is a schematic of a completed EPW. In our first book we take you through the process of building one out from the early days when your objectives and projects will be badly mismatched.

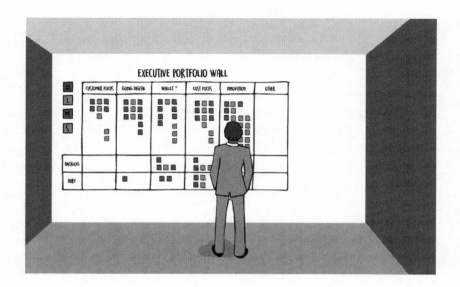

Here though we have reached a good outcome where there is plenty of balance.

The Wall consists of:

- The enterprise's main goals (top line);

- Currently funded projects under each of these, represented by the different coloured Post-its.

- A colour code for size of project (roughly representing cost and duration) - you could also use T Shirt sizes for this.

- A backlog row to indicate work waiting to start (but not yet resourced or held up by work-bottlenecks).

- The Bury row to indicate work that has been cancelled.

Those stickies you see can carry any or all of the information snippets in the large red Post-It, screen right.

This information is all you need to know for a complete overview of all the activity that executives have funded. It also gives you an overview of how well balanced your portfolio is between the main goals of the firm. You might want to add to it some markers of work-in-progress but other than that it is pretty complete.

An important point we make in Flow is that this is our version of an EPW. You might have a different one. You might just copy this version. Flow is not a rules-based system. It is the lightest possible framework for being business agile. And it relies on you taking a creative approach.

Our mantra is simple: good interaction creates good decisions. You cannot interact over things you cannot see so get as much as possible onto a wall. In our first book we explain all the benefits you will get from doing that in the Executive suite and how to lead executives through the process.

How do you encourage Executives to expose their flaws? It takes a senior leader to coax another senior leader into action. Yes, you need buy-in.

STARTING POINTS FOR AN EXECUTIVE PORTFOLIO WALL

This next EPW is a way to lead into the larger canvas. In this Wall we are more focused on the C-Suite's overview of IT and helping senior leaders to understand what IT is achieving for them.

Recently we met with a board member of a major bank. She holds non-executive roles on a number of PLC boards. She talked about the roles and responsibilities of board members and distinguished it from things like IT. IT, she said, was the CIO's responsibility and a board did not need an IT specialist.

Out of politeness we made no comment but nothing could be much further from the truth. Neither executives nor board members have enough IT expertise to make good decisions in a software driven economy. That represents a very big risk. Companies need IT expertise on the board to ensure that executives are taking advantage of all the opportunities presented by IT and to understand the changes modern IT demands of human processes.

Most major organisations have serious legacy issues, which means they have a creaking IT estate that is vulnerable to overload, attack and technical debt. We developed this EPW to help educate the C-Suite about these types of issues.

Executive Portfolio Wall - IT Estate

	Ideation	Feasibility	Ready to Play	In Play	Done
Projects and propositions	▢▢	▢▢▢	▢	▢	▢▢
Mandatory and regulatory		▢	▢▢		▢▢▢
Technical debt and BAU					
Pause		▢			
Kill		▢	▢	▢	▢

In this Wall you can see down the left hand side we are trying to explain to the C-Suite what is happening in three key areas: technical debt, work on regulatory and mandatory projects, and projects and propositions that have a direct impact on customer satisfaction.

Across the top you see a progress board.

- Ideation - a random list of stuff, ideas about what might or might not improve an area (and we do keep it loose!).

- Feasibility - risks explored.

- Ready to Play - units of work awaiting resources.

- In Play - the work has been accepted by IT to start.

This kind of EPW shows executives how much they are committing to meeting obligations; whether or not they are investing enough in the IT estate; and whether or not the outputs they have asked for are actually sitting in idle-mode because they haven't resourced them. As we said above it is a way of educating executives about IT.

Setting up an Executive Portfolio Wall is easy. Getting Executives and Leaders to use it is hard. Very hard. They prefer the security of their offices and the reams of paper churned out by project management offices (PMOs). But they do get used to it.

At first, they appear to be like fish out of water. In reality, they are very smart people who have not experienced business agile practices.

BRIDGING THE IT BUSINESS DIVIDE

The Executive Portfolio Wall is the missing link in Agile. They are the visualisations and the venues that bridge the divides that exist within organisations. You know the problem: too many silos in the executive suite and all through the organisation. But EPWs get people talking across departments. They give new insights. They are fabulously, deceptively simple.

The divisions within companies are traditionally addressed through rules about what people should do and what they are expected to hand over to each other. Or they are addressed through consulting assignments and technologies that cost millions.

Actually what's needed are three simple things:

Insight - literally to see inside the organisation and what is actually going on. That's what the EPW gives you;

Conversation - yes, again literally. People need to talk more about what really matters in value-creation because right now they are busy talking about which rules to follow and who has or who hasn't followed procedure or whether or not a job or report is done or not done. If they can see value processes they can talk about them;

Common language - having said let's talk more, we have to also ensure that the language is well understood. The language of value is not. We can't overstate its importance but that doesn't mean we want you to get uptight about it. Value is a conversation, many conversations. That's all.

This ability to bridge the gaps and divides in the organisation and to enlighten everybody about what is going on is why we believe that Flow Agile is transformative. When coupled with effective Customer Feedback loops (from Focus Groups, Contact Centre incidents or Social Media monitoring) you will have achieved a really powerful, efficient flow from the source of the river to its destination.

CHAPTER 8

Value, The Anti-Plan and Testing

Business is, or should be, about creating value. That sounds wonderfully true and simple. However, plenty of obstacles get in the way. Three of the most significant are:

- We often don't search for value, we look to save on cost.

- We can't truly understand value until we know what customers will buy, enjoy and share (even that is frequently a work-in-progress).

- We plan too much and don't test enough.

Most companies rely on planning as a kind of quality control. But plans are increasingly inflexible for the needs of the day. You cannot be business agile and be a planner. The act of planning creates too much rigidity and takes too much time.

Testing can take up the slack. Testing is misunderstood and maligned. In software environments testing tends to be a big deal at the planning stage of a project (but bear in mind we have to become anti-project). Big test suites are created but are never properly used. In lean startup, by way of contrast, the term used more often than testing is experimentation. There is a happy medium between the old idea of testing in software and the new idea of experimentation. Testing can be a kind of "checking in."

We should always be checking in, running a rule over things, and taking advice from colleagues. Work is a social activity and as Jim McGee said it used to be the norm to work in a public way. When your object is on a lathe it can be seen. Just because the object is virtual, we should not preclude that work from social activity in the workplace.

Creating a good test and iteration culture is entirely in line with the direction business is headed in (and you will see it in our Flow Value Stack). Before you think about a plan, think about how you will test ideas and work-in-progress. Testing culture is a consultative one. We run stuff past people. We get folks together and get a view.

Much of the smart thinking in this area comes from adventurous and creative people in the software domain who have seen through the fallacies of project management and now do social interaction instead. So, in this chapter, we will be looking at the new culture of software testing and draw out lessons for business agility.

In approaching this topic we need to understand that business everywhere is becoming more experimental. There is hardly a business sector not touched by the need for deep change. Experiments imply tests.

So how do we go about becoming serial testers? And what should we be testing? The answer to the latter is value. We need to test for value creation. What about the former?

DON'T LEAN AND AGILE METHODOLOGIES PROVIDE VALUE ANYWAY?

In important methodologies like Lean and Agile, we believe we have tools to assess value when in reality we do not. They promise value but what they really do is give you waste reduction or a road to project completion.

The *best* these methods can do therefore is tell us where resources are being obviously wasted but within the context of projects that may be of great value or no value. They are efficiency methods, not value methods and, importantly, they condition people to think in ways that can be anti-value.

To create value in Lean is to take out cost and to streamline. That creates and perpetuates a culture that priorities only one set of values, waste reduction (or cost savings).

In Agile, value is more elliptical. We know we should build value, because the Agile Manifesto says so, but it is not clear how. There is nothing in Agile methodology to guide us other than to be customer-centric.

While every lean and agile project out there believes it is more efficient than ever, we are often guilty of becoming very efficient at creating little value or even destroying it.

There are many instances when teams work on projects that add very little value, even though they are executed well. The two, efficiency and value creation, do not go hand-in-glove. That point was made to us recently by an executive at the British bank Barclays where for a while teams used **throughput** as a measure of success - in other words more code or more apps done more quickly.

Doing more can mean doing worse but we still obsess over these volume types of metrics. And because we have some kind of metric (a test suite, number of likes, Twitter retweets) we believe we are judging value when in fact we could be judging only volume.

The job of value-seeking behaviour at work is to seek those features and functions that create a better customer experience. We believe this to be driven by a broad set of activities. It is about seeking out what customers want but it is also about doing this in a way that priorities visualisation, so we can harness collective intelligence, and developing social interaction so that the collective voice gets a good hearing.

To ensure that the work you commission or execute is adding value to customers, you need to take this multifaceted approach (see Chapter 6) and you need value-seeking to become an embedded behaviour. It has to be a value in its own right. When it is, you will find that some of your treasured processes become irrelevant.

QUALITY TESTING VS VALUE TESTING

When you look at value in a multifaceted way it forces you rethink how you test for quality.

In point of fact, it forces you to do a lot more. You need to reappraise many team roles too. The idea of a "multidisciplinary team" is the wrong term for this as everybody has to become multidisciplinary. The role of digital marketer epitomises this. A good digital marketer will know web design, SEO, content creation and A/B testing. Being multidisciplinary is not a feature of the team but of everyone's role within it. In software that is true of developers and testers (their roles can be interchangeable) and BAs and product owners. We are fast moving towards fungible roles where we can, thankfully, break out of the personal silos created by HR policies.

But back to quality. At the very least you need to know that work is not just of high quality but is actually creating value. You'd be surprised how that simple idea gets distorted in many organisations.

Most organisations have a cadence to their work. For example writing up a project proposal for executive approval might be regarded as a three week's long task. In our experience good proposals can be generated in a couple of hours but that doesn't stop a product owner from taking the project off on a three week tour!

This cadence of activity, the "what's expected" approach to innovation, is killing companies in the West. it is irrelevant to many Chinese companies who are anyway innovating all the time. Testing belongs in this group of extremely long processes that could really be knocked off a lot more quickly. To understand this we should distinguish between quality and testing. Traditionally we thought of testing as a quality control method. But if we think about that a little longer, should it not be a value-testing tool? High quality work that has no value is still bad work.

We got talking about the quality v testing problem with Alan Murphy who has a major role to play in defining quality at Paddy Power, one of the stars of DevOps and Flow.

Paddy Power is not an untypical digital company. It has a "bricks and mortar" presence on many High Streets but the real power of the company lies in its ability to create new digital products on the fly. By the way, we are assuming you are familiar with this ability. Paddy Power manages 7 million prices changes every Saturday afternoon during the soccer season and pushes out new products (in this case bets) all through the day.

Alan Murphy specialises in changing the company's approach to software quality control and is passionate about it. He is a good person to talk with about the issue of quality and value.

Above everything else, Alan is passionate about **_unit testing_**. Unit testing is distinct from the traditional software testing regime. But what does testing software matter to marketers or other people in the business?

In software, test suites are usually drawn up at the beginning of a project or a significant sprint. What makes this analogous to other parts of the business is that testers are expected to anticipate everything that might be relevant weeks or months down the road and plan their tests accordingly.

Because, in reality, nobody can do this, it leads to a very curious outcome. Many projects fail their acceptance tests and are put into production anyway!

Our belief in the power to plan is reflected in a whole range of projects that executives commission or buy. Even the act of digital transformation is a big plan.

As we move towards smaller units of work across the business, testing in a granular way (by the unit of work) becomes more relevant. As we move, towards a more experimental enterprise, testing itself becomes a cultural necessity.

You might argue that there is some overkill in testing so much. But new disciplines in software, like DevOps, mean that work has to be reorganised to facilitate speed. Companies grind to a halt when bad work is let through to the public and then has to be reworked. Testing becomes more important and more relevant even to getting things done fast.

As with all the other elements of Flow we believe the principles apply to all areas of a company's work.

Very often we work alongside colleagues who claim a special degree of expertise and won't be challenged (or put another way, won't be tested). They can be pretty vocal about what they know to be true.

That kind of attitude could come from, say, copywriters who are responsible for generating website content. Their traditional role was to be the creative. Companies relied on their intuitive feel for words and audiences. Now, however, we can test most content to see what type of audience it attracts. And we can also apply some rules or guidelines to content in order to maximise its searchability. Following on from that we can continue to test whether Google is responding in the way we expect or if we have to add more visual content and so on. Creative work is becoming more testable.

So while Alan talks about software testing, the lessons are applicable to other digital skill areas.

MANAGERS FAIL TO REALISE THE BENEFITS OF TESTING

The big issue for the unit testing advocate is that management generally sees unit testing as a waste of time and an activity that holds up coding (the old throughput mentality). This is less the case in marketing where the numbers have assumed too much importance. But it is nonetheless interesting to note that other departments are leading the charge in testing everything.

"Managers and other stakeholders perceive unit testing as adding cost," says Alan, "but that idea, and the elimination of unit testing, is a completely false economy because you will be breaking something in production later and then you will have to fix it in production rather than in development.

It is very easy to look efficient by pushing code into production quickly but it will just be coming right back at you as bugs.

There's also a tendency to allocate test writing to inexperienced developers, often people who are young and new to the company, who you are asking to write quite complex test suites for acceptance testing. It never, never works and it always ends up needing more development work. When you have broad unit testing coverage you can blaze into production with very small changes and very little blowback.

THE TESTING ENVIRONMENT

Unit testing is made possible because Flow teams break work down into very small units. In Paddy Power that meant 3-5 day units, though now Fin works in 2 day units, and shorter if possible.

Mastercard recently revealed that they allow a 12 hour window to respond to micro trends!!

Small units of work are very relevant to DevOps. Because DevOps incentivises getting work right as it goes into production rather than reworking later, you need methods that ensure quality as far upstream as possible. That's what unit testing gives you.

Now imagine the equivalent in marketing. A piece of copy has been signed off at the product manager level but as it goes into the company's different channels it looks as though the content is witty and wonderful in print but is very poorly optimised for SEO, so poorly optimised that the likely knock on effect will be either poor uptake of a feature or the need to secure extra budget for search engine marketing (SEM). Bidding for keywords can be ruinously expensive so getting the text right for SEO is materially important.

This kind of copywriting project needed breaking down into small units of work, just like modern software. It will go into different environments so it needs to be optimised for each and often it will have to be optimised quickly (see Mastercard above. You have a 12 hour window to create code, text and offer!). We can learn a lot from our software colleagues.

Similar challenges exist throughout the organisation. Distribution of products used to belong the the culture of large systems. Big orders from big wholesalers or supermarkets or retail chains. Big delivery schedules for big lorries. But that too is changing. Far and away the fastest growing area of logistics over the past two decades is parcel delivery. That trend will continue as platforms like Alibaba come to dominate a greater portion of global trade. Managing multiple small orders is tough. If you are serving microtrends of between 12 hours and three days then logistics systems have to be ready to adapt quickly too. Event-days like China's Singles Days or Amazon Prime pose huge problems of managing massive numbers of small items. The capacity to think small has never been so important.

Testing systems, processes, features, copy, strategy and so on is very important and Alan's point is that these tests are best carried out on the fly rather than at the end of a process set-up. You want a test mentality that prevents a complete reworking of any given system.

According to Alan, a unit resting approach creates a unique test-driven environment.

> *"We allied unit testing with acceptance testing and really departed from industry standards when we did that, as well as by getting the developer to code the test. We have a just-in-time discussion of acceptance criteria but very lightweight. We quickly convene the product owner, tester and developer, build up 4 or 5 use cases and ask the simple questions, given x, when y, then z should happen. Does it?"*

Just-in-time acceptance testing can be applied anywhere. The example we gave above of Mastercard's 12 hour turnaround is ideally suited to rapid just-in-time methods that create, test and deliver at exceptional speed. It is only possible when you create small units of work. J-I-T acceptance testing means you are more likely to be testing work of value. Those 4 or 5 use cases are a checkpoint for work-of-value not just quality and acceptance. And in good organisations the developer takes on a bigger role - querying whether a unit of work actually creates value.

CHANGING ROLES

Redesigning work practices, often on the fly, comes with a cost. It causes a lot of friction because people need to learn new roles and redefine their personal boundaries. Outside the IT shop marketers, logistics and distribution as well as inbound supply chains will be going through the same changes.

The analogy in marketing would be the introduction of search engine marketing and search engine optimisation and then from there, the introduction of social media. All of these developments have forced marketers to continuously develop their skills and roles, and to introduce data on performance that simply was not available in the old days. They have become testers of their own performance through analytics programs and A/B tests.

That process could be taken further, faster. Although marketers do more of this with their online content than they used to, we believe there is still a long way to go before they truly pass the Flow test. They need to segment their markets more, broaden and diversify product offerings and create more real-time units of work across the long-tail of customers.

The priority is to get to the stage where testing your ideas, designs, and systems becomes a regular social event often convened just-in-time.

There is a reluctance to see routine testing as central to all this. Testing, done properly, can replace planning.

"One of the biggest inhibitors to unit testing is developer ignorance," Alan says. *"Developers haven't been exposed to this type of thinking. Testing has been treated as a separate discipline."*

It has to become part of daily practice. Like chatting about segmentation at the Customer Innovation Wall, conversing over work breakdown, convening a few folks to test ideas, features or insights, all work is a regular conversation.

WHY WE SHOULD BE ANTI-PROJECT

Some of the grief that comes with change is also caused by confusion in old upstream roles. Product owners need to reappraise how they work but so too do product managers. Yet, the most difficult work structure for Flow practitioners is the project, bailiwick of project managers.

Projects get green lights from far off, they get a budget and momentum and that makes them almost like a missile screaming through the business: they are unstoppable. They resist all the logic of small units of work and unit testing because they have been mandated. They have to be completed.

In IT it is becoming obvious that a traditional approach to projects is failing. Some of that is attributable to the way testing is organised as a project. Thinking in units of work and in regular testing is a better way to go, whether you are in IT, marketing, logistics or finance.

Here is the summary of our conversation with Alan, mixed in with some of our own observations about quality, testing and value. It very much applies directly to IT but we will finish off the chapter by applying it elsewhere.

1. Traditional testing suites bite off more than they can chew, as do traditional plans of all kinds. They test a matrix of code that, in reality, is too complex to test. Very often code will not pass acceptance yet because of time pressures, still go into production, fully compromised!

2. Code often gets pushed into production too early and conflict between development and production goes up another notch.

3. This is partly because, traditionally, work was considered "done", in agile terms, too far up the value chain when we don't know if it will be adding value or if it functions properly in the wider project. Work is not done until you have evidence it has value and that usually means once a customer has used it and provide feedback.

4. This brings IT much closer to other areas of the business like marketing and provides the basis for cooperation.

5. Unit tests can be coupled to just-in-time acceptance tests that are a rough and ready consensus that work meets our current understanding of customer requirements. Those J-I-T tests are another way of building cooperation.

6. Unit testing is what really makes DevOps work; it's what allows you to blaze code into production with minimal changes.

7. Units of work are the smallest unit you can break work down to.

8. Good practice should involve a broad coverage of unit testing.

9. Unit testing is applicable across all work in all departments.

10. It should also involve developers challenging product owners about the value of any increment of work; given a unit of work as a responsibility a developer can ask cogent questions about its value to business outcomes.

11. That means everyone is focused on value.

12. It also forces a continuous reevaluation of key roles like product owner, product manager, project manager.

So those are the key points of Alan's experience.

APPLYING THE IDEA OF TESTING RATHER THAN PLANNING IN AN AGILE BUSINESS

How can these experiences and thoughts be applied outside IT? We already touched on that above with respect to content and SEO. But there are numerous other ways. In Flow, the first book, we pointed out the temptation on the part of many executives to buy big projects either from external vendors or from internal champions. The problem of big projects is that they push value too far into the future, so far that sometimes the original champions leave well before value becomes questionable.

And they rely on exemplary use-cases - such as company A did this and saved $10 million. Very little in those use-cases is tested or testable in a way that would support decision making.

In addition nobody should forget that everything in business is trending towards small. In the financial sector, as an example, banks are looking to Fintech startups for inspiration on what to change and how. Software systems are trending towards microservices that communicate with each other. Marketing is no longer about TV ads, print and outdoor. It has to take into account Snapchat, as well as Facebook and Google, Pinterest, bloggers and influencers. These are all smaller initiatives compared with anything from the past and they carry just as much scope for testing at a small scale as software does.

We are even seeing the most dramatic system changes taking place because of the skills and passions of small companies. In the financial space the ICO or Initial Coin Offering has changed the way funding is raised for startups. This is a product of small companies but it is changing how we view value-creation.

In insurance, we have given the example of drones. Drones are a game-changer for insurers both as a forensic device, allowing them to take an aerial view of any damage, often in locations that assessors cannot properly reach, and also in disaster response.

The use of drones introduces new system requirements such as drone fleet management. Unlike car and van fleet management, drone fleet management is a real time interactive activity. Somebody has to steer the drones from a distance.

Nobody knows how to design drone fleet management routines. It is entirely a matter of trial and error, or test-and-see. That's why insurers work with small specialist companies that are amassing this test experience from multiple projects. The principles of experimentation or testing are entering every sphere of business. We believe that the Flow technique of small units of work tested at the point of acceptance is a good model for testing, and hence innovation, everywhere.

What you can also see from this short description is that new roles are inevitable. There was no such thing as a drone fleet manager 10 years ago; not even three years ago. But it will become more commonplace. There are no "testers" or "test writers" in many areas of business. There are QA people who have a role in ensuring that technologies meet a particular performance threshold. But we believe testing will become a specific function across the business some time very soon.

CHAPTER 9

Reinventing Roles

In Flow, we believe in multidisciplinary people. Multidisciplinary teams are great but life is better when people step up and fill roles well beyond those on their job description. Many areas of work life are very novel, a point we don't need to reiterate too much here. Not much can get done if people insist on doing just what they were hired for.

A problem that many organisations encounter with business agile can be traced back to the confusion they have created around significant roles, though. We are living through rapid change and what made sense last month might not make sense now. That's particularly the case with what we expect of people.

That expectation is pivotal in a number of ways and one is the business-IT divide. Multidisciplinary people do not see this divide. They are accomplished, to a degree, at some business skill (say digital marketing) and at understanding what IT can achieve. We will say more about this in Chapter 11 when we talk about personal development goals and in the Epilogue. But there is a reason to introduce it now.

In this chapter we are going to talk about new roles and how to encourage the development of multidisciplinary people. Critical to this process is to eliminate the gap between product managers (who tend to be based in marketing) and product owners (who tend to be based in IT).

Before going into that, let's once again emphasise that the solution is people-oriented. A point we make in Flow is that you cannot buy digital transformation as a platform or technology. Digital transformation, in general, requires people to transform how they see themselves in work, why they show up and how they perform. To get people into these new mindsets requires a relationship skill or a set of relationship skills and the desire to seek value. There isn't a piece of software for it.

You can define roles clearly and enthusiastically only to find they are becoming less relevant as your organisation finds out more about the challenges of continuous innovation.

Plenty of organisations have people allocated to each important function that's been defined as essential to success. But they have neither defined all functions well, nor understood the direction of change and its most important consequence - people need to perform a number of roles interchangeably because even clear role definitions will be subject to change.

Examples include social media experts and software test writers.

The arrival of social media created a lot of menial work that people could not embrace. Tweeting on behalf of a client can be a career entry path in an ad agency but let's face it, the work is empty. Yet people are held in these roles for months, if not years. In the modern workplace they could become much more pivotal to a fully digital team, taking on the role of product owner to parse their understanding of customer conversation to analysts. But hey! Who's to say that they can't also fulfil the role of analyst or get involved in a j-i-t acceptance test too. The fact is people who have social media skills are underused. Doing social media is a fragment of the knowledge they hold. They know who influences people; they know analytics; they could segment audiences in fresh ways and be a font of inspiration on unexpected customer reactions. Sadly, their role is not defined that way.

Software testing has a similar issue to resolve. Test suites are usually written by inexperienced developers. Because testing is undervalued, the work is given to people who are generally new and need projects to cut their teeth on. The result is that quality is often seriously compromised because developers cannot meet the shaky test requirements. The software has to be pushed through to production or the project risks becoming an overrun. In effect, the firm allows itself to be held captive to inexperience.

In short, companies are stuck with role rigidity, poor role definition and role mismatch when they should be freeing people to fungibility and value-seeking behaviour.

Even companies that appear to be performing well suffer these problems. We're going to argue, in this chapter, that unless you get this area right you will not transform and nor will you be efficient and productive in the sense we defined elsewhere. Key to this is transforming the product owner into a catalyst for value. To understand why that is not the case, let's look first at a typical workflow and its dangers.

A TYPICAL, BROKEN WORKFLOW

The place of the IT department within an organisation varies greatly. In some cases there is a clear business-IT divide. The workflow creates that divide. Usually a product manager and his or her team, will create a set of requirements for a product and hand this over to the IT team who will place it into backlog until the resources are available to begin development.

A business analyst will usually break that project down so that any development effort is shaped around business rules and business logic. These are quite simple rules that keep a project within the framework of a company's prices, policies and terms and conditions while the logic is a description of the workflow: how the new feature will flow through the organisation.

At that point the requirements of people in marketing, say, are more or less transformed into an IT project.

In the next phase, developers will work away in different sprint teams. When they are finished with their sprint, they will try to integrate disparate work units into something tangible and, hopefully, fault-free to pass on to the operations team.

Much of that work will be poorly integrated, because different teams may have taken a slightly different approach. It will have passed through a test-system that often is not capable of spotting problems because the testing procedure will be designed weeks in advance with no way to anticipate changes to the original plan. These will surface later in call-centre complaints or poor uptake of a product or feature online.

The handover from business to IT, the work of the analyst, the integration of code from different scrum teams, the testing process, poor integration, all present handover conflict points. Much of the inflexibility inside organisations can be traced back to conflict. Different teams within the organisation don't necessarily get on. They are suspicious of each other or they resent having to compensate for poor work further upstream. That's one more reason why we emphasise the importance of good social interaction.

Adding to the potential for conflict is the fact that the IT team may been forced to follow the business plan rigidly, even when it becomes apparent that the business goals have been wrongly framed. This set of difficulties is the norm and as we already said, the potential harm that human conflict does to quality and value is an overlooked factor.

We said in an earlier chapter that there are missing ingredients here that the scrum agile framework doesn't necessarily provide guidance on. Conflict is a feature of the handover process, which is why, at the operations end of IT, DevOps emerged - to integrate development, testing and operations. But even in DevOps, the formal transformation of a requirement into a project creates all kinds of artificial boundaries that make high performance difficult to achieve.

What you really want in an enterprise is for business goals to be adaptive and for these to iterate as IT experience of delivering them grows, as described in Chapter 5.

The pivotal role of the product owner is to mediate between the experiences of trying to develop a product or feature and the goals that are driving it.

Traditionally, if there is such a thing in Agile, the product owner would create the requirement that would then be handed on to the developer team, with some conversation about the vision alongside it.

However, when you operate with small units of work this changes. The priority becomes the iteration cycle above. Breaking the work down to small units, getting some experience with coding them, running some rough tests on their acceptability, gathering customer feedback and then seeing how those impact the business goals. This is the best way to create value as distinct from delivering a project.

And being adaptive means making "pivot" decisions at the last possible point of commitment. We prefer to think of this as iterative experimentation rather than fail-fast, fail-cheap, by the way.

AN EXAMPLE OF APPLYING THE FLEXIBLE GOALS MANTRA

You may have a requirement to undertake a survey through a website, as we describe earlier in the book. Integrating the survey into the digital flow is the product owner's job as the survey relates to a range of potential new features of services the business is planning.

The main business goal is to understand customer needs in a way that helps shape feature design. Specifically it is "to understand customer needs in specific segments." A few features that have gone through to customers recently have suffered poor uptake so some insight is needed in order to get better value from work. The team have realised that design is too divorced from the customer feedback loop, so they are making a special effort to become better informed. However, the backlog is full and resources are scarce.

Now the product owner has a choice. The survey idea in a traditional form could just take too long and the lack of resources presents an opportunity to experiment. The answer is to go for speed. The goal of creating more understanding could be done better and quicker by developing a set of interactions that would play out via Twitter: or a Twitter survey (a favourite example of ours you may have noticed).

In Flow we want to get work done in small units and two-day cycles so she decides the Twitter option gives her a way to stimulate the web team with a challenging project (always gamify when you can) and can be squeezed into the backlog much more easily than a larger survey. All this gives her a chance to get hold of the additional data she needs if she is going to persuade her marketing colleagues and IT colleagues that a pivot is needed in feature design.

This does mean that the business goal is not fully achievable in its original form. Based on previous experience in IT a flow of insights, however, is better than a formal report that ends up needing various levels of sign-off. The pivot to a Twitter-based survey is cheap enough that she can repeat it several times. The key though is pivoting the business goal. it will no longer be "understanding customer needs in specific segments." It will be "a snapshot of customer commentary to keep product design fresh."

Weighing the benefits of speed against comprehensiveness and depth is important. Projects that take months often get forgotten or buried in the frenetic clamour for resources. Securing some value after two days or a week, and doing that multiple times throughout the organisation, creates a completely different culture. People don't get to hide within a slow or traditional cadence of work. They have to be more out there, reporting on the value of what they have done.

Without the capacity to change the business requirement you really have no grasp of where value lies.

The pivot also arises from real interaction between the different experiences of the overall team, which is way better for morale and might produce a result that people buy into more easily. Social interaction is a key component of it.

The point is that the product owner's job is to deliver value within the context of an adaptive business goal. The job is not to complete multiple projects where value is hidden for weeks and months.

The product owner has to move away from a rigid product requirement or a fixed goal to something far more adaptive. To empower her to do that is to empower everyone else to become value-seeking too. The product owner leads the charge.

THE END OF THE OLD AGILE PRODUCT OWNER

The fit between business goals and a unit of work in IT needs flexibility or we all revert to fulfilling our obligations rather than setting out to find value.

Scrum Agile is becoming more adaptive in this area. Sprints used to be fixed and unchangeable but recently changes have been allowed as long as the Sprint Goals remain constant. In reality what we are often talking about however is "Wagile" at best. Even with more adaptability, Agile is not flexible enough.

Scrum operates in relatively large units of work and arguably fails to incorporate enough different skills. It encourages holistic teams but our point is that the team needs multidisciplinary people, those who can set up a just-in-time acceptance test as well as contribute to work breakdown as well as being savvy about how value is emerging and what it takes to grow it.

It is also important to realise that very few organisations have created a role that champions flexibility. In our view that champion is a different kind of product owner than exists today.

Often a product owner has more of a product manager role and sees his job as curating the product rather than changing it, prolonging the status quo rather than taking a chance on something new. That person can become a blocker. However, more often than not, the blocker is the lack of clarity and inappropriate role definition. There are product owners who are never really clear about the value they should be seeking and adding. The confusion over these roles needs clearing up.

Let's look at a definition. In Scrum Agile the product owner plays a pivotal role in the relationship between IT and the business, or at least she should.

"The Scrum product owner is typically a project's key stakeholder. Part of the product owner responsibilities is to have a vision of what he or she wishes to build, and convey that vision to the scrum team. This is key to successfully starting any agile software development project."

In the best examples of Agile, the product owner is a match-maker between a team and customers and users, and also a figure of authority that can manage internal politics. But this is a good case. There are many instances where the product owner is less influential and is more of a proxy for customers rather than a matchmaker.

There is nothing intrinsically wrong with that. But its effect is that somebody gets the title product owner without being offered all the professional development needed to fulfil those roles and is then plonked in the middle of a relationship that has been fractious for a long time. The product owner sits in the IT-Business divide.

Very few, in our experience, have significant insights into marketing and customers, beyond the reductionist practice of creating personas.

In reality that product owner either ends up coming from a marketing background and therefore tends not to understand IT, does not know what it is capable of delivering, and can even be aloof from IT; or the product owner comes from an IT background and simply does not know enough about business.

Having product owners from one side or the other does not solve a big relationship problem. It just means you now have somebody to carry the can.

It's worth mentioning here too that a product owner can be responsible for agreeing the changes to a requirement prior to a team going into a new sprint. The product owner or Scrum Master becomes the key to unblocking old Waterfall work methods. But we pointed out elsewhere that many of the problems of Waterfall persist.

Lean techniques like MVPs can introduce even more suspicion. Product managers think of the idea of a minimal viable product as a minimal commitment to delivery. As a consequence they overfill their requirements with features, sure (!) that IT will jettison essential development tasks in order to keep work to a minimum.

These issues arose out of an attempt to solve an old set of problems. In the context of monolithic projects they created a mechanism for managing conflicts where no mechanism existed before. They made somebody responsible for establishing some kind of order, truce, fixed point of stability, call it what you will.

But this was always a vague role and doesn't work as well as hoped. It is no longer so relevant when the whole system of creating value is open to change. We are moving to environments where multiple innovations occur every day and therefore we need roles, skills and relationships that fit with the tensions and creativity caused by a constant flow of innovation.

We need developers who understand more about the business and how it is changing into a matrix of shifting feature priorities, as well as knowing users and value creation.

If we are going to have product managers they need to be people who understand what capabilities IT now has, so they know how to get the most out of it for customers.

They need to understand the sources of feedback data and what it can tell the team about new features and functions; they need to be able to spot ecosystem activity that can be nurtured; and microtrends that offer immediate opportunities. In short, we think this new product owner should be a value-discovery agent.

FROM PRODUCT OWNER TO FLOW VALUE MANAGER

The product owner role came to prominence because of Agile methodology, which assigns him or her responsibilities such as product definition and vision, backlog grooming and stakeholder relationships. But a role defined by IT culture is not likely to perform well across the whole business. In fact, if you look at what product owners really should be doing, you start to realise the concept needs to change. Firms would be better off redesigning the role as a value manager who is skilled enough to orchestrate the growth of value across product life cycles.

A good value manager should understand the coding and operational environment and also be very cognisant of marketing requirements - after all an increasing amount of marketing goes through the IT shop to a website. - She should bringing a good knowledge of customer needs into the equation. That doesn't happen as often as it should because IT, like marketing, is over-dependent on hunches about personas rather than seeking out real needs.

A good product owner or value manager should also be able to support the work breakdown process. They and business analysts are critical to translation of business goals into units of work. There is also a testing component of the role.

Very often a value manager will be an excellent business analyst and by excellent we mean capable of changing business goals when necessary and managing those changes up the hierarchy. The most overlooked skill of all is knowing when business goals have to change or when a project can be unblocked by being flexible about goals. That means product owners have to dedicate themselves to uncovering value.

In software-driven companies marketing is actually an IT-driven task. It is integral to the real-time assessment of a product or feature. That means the product owner or value manager has to master social data, analytics, call-centre data, trend insights, conversion performance, DevOps capabilities, backlog management, UX experience, application usage and so on.

The new skill set is summarised below. You can see straight away that it is a role for more than one person or a role for one person with tremendous variety in their background.

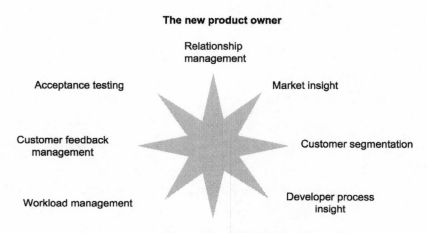

We talk later about new personal development goals and how to curate your own goals in a personal learning management system. But first here is a summary of new product owner skills. There is an important caveat here of course. Everyone should be able to take on the role of product owner!

Relationship management - Where was that two-day course when you needed it! Knowing how to manage the expectations of disparate groups is a key art but very little in the way of training exists. Our advice - authenticity. Don't go out there trying to please people. Get the focus on value and be mildly relentless about it. We're all here to create value so keep that in front of people without berating them.

Customer segmentation - Companies pay too little attention to segments and their needs. In the long-tail economy this is disastrous, so product owners need to get onto it.

Market analysis - Good customer segmentation can often be achieved with social listening tools. Market insight is an additional ingredient. It includes competitor analysis but the real key insight today is how and why people share. Sharing needs to be built into product design. It's a new asset and rarely developed to its full extent.

Developer process insight - Understanding how IT processes are changing is critical to raising the ambition levels of the business. Listen in as IT shifts over to DevOps and microservices or pulls in some low code skills.

Requirements setting and goal management - It is a traditional area but how good are you? In Flow we think of requirements as goals that get broken into those small units we keep talking about. Goal management is critical to getting the right work done.

Workload management - A product owner has to get products into the development process so having an eye for workload makes a whole lot of sense. Fin prefers his product owners embedded with the developer team so that they intuitively know where the pressures are and when an opportunity to introduce new work will crop up.

Real time customer feedback management - Pulling data from the call centres, social listening tools, customer labs, surveys and conversations all tell you what you are doing right and wrong.

Acceptance testing - Be prepared to play a role in activities like acceptance tests, just-in-time.

Real-time feedback loops are also an important feature of the overall flow of value and the role of the product owner/business analyst. What are those loops?

1. *Real-time analytics* from call-centres (this is much easier now that companies are introducing call-centre bots).

2.   ***Real-time web analytics*** (assessments of where people
       come to when they arrive at your site, the pages they visit,
       the time they spend on a page, the actions they take).

3.   ***Real-time usage analytics*** (many products now have a
       data gathering function and can provide real-time usage
       data).

4.   ***Real time social media analytics*** (data from social media
       sources providing a real-time insight into what people are
       saying about you).

5.   ***Sharing behaviour*** (who shares your products or infor-
       mation with whom?)

In the system we have described over the previous eight steps,
however, you'll note we have also emphasised:

No projects - a move away from thinking about projects with a
traditional beginning, middle, end milestone and deliverable.

No estimates & no budgets - there is a burgeoning movement
away from the incessant obsession with estimating, budgeting &
forecasting by armies of finance/governance teams trying to justify
their existence. In Flow, with consistent cycle-times, you just count
the Post-Its on a project or Kanban Wall to arrive at your estimates
& forecasts. As for budgets, if you feed the team the most valuable
things to work on, you'll reap the return on investment or pivot
quickly to look elsewhere.

Very small units of work - 1-2 day units of work that encourage people to bring work back to the Wall very often and therefore
encourage social interaction.

Co-creating processes - highly visual work breakdown where as
many people as necessary engage in defining priorities and how an
objective should be reached (the process and tools).

Informality - frequent informal acceptance agreements so that work can be kept moving.

Value-seeking behaviour - using multiple strategies to question if work has value and how value can be increased.

Experimentation - using hypothesis about what might add value and finding a way to test these, usually by pushing a matrix of features through to customers before committing to full development of any one of those features.

Not many companies set themselves up to deal with these challenges or to get somebody to champion solutions to them. It's high time that they invested in a new type of person, not one from IT or marketing but someone with an eye on value.

And what about the Scrum Master? The role is quite often taken by project managers or "Jira Jockeys" as Fin calls them, which is why everything becomes very task driven. Since we wrote Flow some people are talk about Flow Masters (we prefer the term Flow Ambassadors). But in Flow we think that it's everyone's job to deliver value. The new product owner has to lead that charge. But it looks likely that the idea of a product owner will change and we will instead have multiple, multi-skilled flow organisers and orchestrators whose key role is value management.

CHAPTER 10

The Customer Feedback Wall

Back in Chapter 2 we discussed improving market segmentation in a very customer-centric way. The Flow Customer Feedback Wall is an additional powerful tool for bringing different parts of the business together in search of customer success. It is a venue for everybody to observe customer opinions and to participate in discussions about what has value for them. It provides inputs for all functions, including strategy.

The idea of customer-centricity is fairly commonplace, as is a "customer-centric architecture". The motive behind it is often: "how can we sell more to them." Firms drag customer-centricity right back into the old habits of sales and marketing targets and techniques. Very often "customer service" or the call center is the price you pay for mis-sold or inappropriate goods.

A different perspective is to regard the customer as a beacon for personalisation or the Amazon-style "market-of-one". But this too has problems. It becomes just another way of framing the cross-sell! And to date, it is not really within reach.

In Flow we advocate authenticity in customer-centric design. In a moment we will go into how the Customer Feedback Wall can help with this, but first a few more words about customer-centricity.

THREE ADDITIONAL ELEMENTS OF CUSTOMER-CENTRICITY

In Flow we are talking with as much authenticity as possible about using the customer-voice to build better products, features and relationships. In many SaaS environments this is now a vibrant discipline in its own right and is referred to as customer success.

How do we go about it in Flow? Mostly through the Customer Innovation Wall and the Customer Feedback Wall but here are three other thoughts.

- Customer labs.

- The Hack Box (for internal entrepreneurs).

- Awareness of SaaS developments, especially their metrics.

CUSTOMER LABS

At Aviva, where Fin now works, developers have constant access to customers through the Customer Lab. People are invited into the lab in order to review new products, features and product ideas. It is exactly what it says: a place to interact with customers in an experimental environment. It is one check on the tendency for companies to develop what they think customers want and then spend a small fortune trying to convince customers to buy.

In fact, at Aviva they use Design Thinking and Design Sprints. These techniques give the team a shortcut to learning without having to build and launch a new proposition.

THE HACK BOX

A related idea is The Hack Box. In place of old hackathons or moonshot programs, The Hack Box is a simple invite to individuals and teams to bring a new product idea forward and get a modest amount of resources to test and iterate ideas that are demonstrably value-adding for customers. It gives employees a chance to take a small step towards a bigger strategic product or proposition with customers baked in.

The box contains guidance on how to use things such as the Business Model Canvas and some seed money to test ideas with customers. An associated training and mentoring program guides employees towards being "Intrapreneurs" and helps them to develop relevant propositions for the Insurance business.

Almost the same way that external disruptors would approach attacking the Insurance value chain. It's the lean startup but within the enterprise.

SAAS METRICS

The software as a service community is a great learning pool for the regular enterprise. SaaS companies have to compete, often with limited budgets in their early days, against all the major platforms around the world. They have to be customer-centric. It is a do or die issue. That means their stock-in-trade is extremely strong user experiences. However, it is in the area of the customer success philosophy and customer success metrics that SaaS platforms have so much to teach.

SaaS companies have pioneered a new generation of key performance indicators and predictive analytics. The basic proposition is that any customer-centric platform will improve the potential of the customer to succeed in some way. It won't just meet a pain point, it will turn the pain point into a strength. There's a great discussion of this over on Hubspot.

But let's go with an example. Haydn is a subscriber to a very popular photo stock site with a subscription of approximately $25 per month. In terms of normal metrics he is a good customer. He has signed up, used it fully for three months but has since barely visited. Same goes for one of their photo enhancement software packages. A good SaaS service would note this lack of use. If this is a common pattern across multiple members then it poses dangers:

1.   The first is that he is waiting for the 12 month obligation to run out when he will end the subscription

2.   The second is that he will begin to complain to friends about the cost of the site and the inflexible subscription policy.

3.   The third is that he has stopped being a potential sharer and advocate of the service and now sees it as a negative experience.

These factors will add to the site's churn and increase the likelihood of exposing it as a fundamentally empty service. It provides photos but it does nothing else. It does not create community nor does it engage its users.

That company is clearly either not measuring usage or is immune to the dangers of non-use and the lost opportunity for advocacy. In many businesses, marketing strategy does not get beyond the concept of recurring revenue. It fails to address the churn problem with proactive service and it loses the chance to become "viral". To date, over a six month period, there has been no opportunity for the customer to voice an opinion. Having made the sale, the vendor is sitting back counting the money. But it is potentially alienating people who could be friends.

Beyond pointing out these important success factors, SaaS models can also teach us plenty about predictive metrics. While many marketing organisations measure sales growth, a more significant metric is the growth in inbound queries. If inbound inquiries are going up, the chances are, sales growth will follow. If they are static or declining then that metric alone signals a need to improve service provision.

THE CUSTOMER FEEDBACK WALL

The most important way to bring customers closer into your business is by integrating the customer's voice into all aspects of design, development and strategy.

Some startups, but by no means all, take this approach because they need quick and accurate feedback about value (they don't have huge investment capacity, after all). The vision and purpose of good startups should be firmly centered on customer value, a relentless focus on customer experience and real-time feedback.

The Customer Feedback Wall allows larger companies can do just that and begin to cultivate the startup adaptability they need.

The Customer Feedback Wall has another value we referred to in Chapter 2. It can be used to direct customer feelings to any department or team and/or to unite teams around live customer concerns. The diagram below shows a customer feedback wall in use for IT and strategy. But there is every reason to include additional columns such as "Assigned to Messaging" to direct customer concerns to social media teams or "Assigned to Logistics" to deal with delivery issues. The only reason we have constrained it is so that it will fit on a page!

In the Feedback Wall here, the target for the feedback is the digital and IT team. By explaining the columns that follow we can tell you how those pain points are dealt with at every level of development and strategy where the digital team's relationship with customers is the focus.

The Customer Feedback Wall

Pain Points	Backlog	Valuation and evaluation	No Change required	Assigned to digital teams	Assigned to core teams	Assigned to process change (systems thinking)	Assigned back to portfolio wall	Let customer know
□□□ □□ □	□ □ □ □	□ □ □	□	□□ □	□□	□	□ □	
Done				□ □	□			

If you were designing a Customer Feedback Wall for marketing it might have columns such as:

Pain points	Backlog	Priorisation and valuation	Assigned to pricing team	Assigned to brand team	Assigned to messaging team	Assigned to IT	Back to Portfolio Wall

In fact every company should have a Customer Feedback Wall for marketing. It is also possible to design the flow specifically to bring different departments together.

Pain points	Backlog	Priorisation and valuation	Assigned to pricing team	Assigned to digital team	Assigned to process change	Assigned working group	Back to Portfolio Wall

So let's go through the columns in the IT-centered Customer Feedback Wall.

IDENTIFYING THE PAIN POINTS

How do we collect customer pain points? There are a variety of sources.

- Customers leave reviews (sometimes just star scores) on a website. That's valuable information, especially if they have gone to the trouble of writing down their comments.

- Then there are telephone calls into the contact/call centres, which again are very valuable data. People have gone to the trouble of telling you what they want to see changed.

- Social media listening is also valuable. Every organisation has access to listening tools and sentiment analysis. Especially from channels such as Twitter. You also have data from your customer lab, from Google or other analytics packages, and the analysis of when customers drop out of a sign-up process or on-line customer journey.

- Other data exists in how people navigate or drop out of your online properties.

This amounts to a pretty comprehensive set of insights as to what customers find difficult about you. There are times as well when it tells you what you are doing right. The negatives though need to be embraced because they tell you how to save money or how to serve customers better, modify products/propositions and make more money. And of course someone needs to be assigned this task.

PRIORITISING THE BACKLOG OF WORK

You need a system to score pain points so that you can set priorities for the backlog of work. That can be as simple as taking the percentage of times that a particular complaint comes up. If more customers are complaining, better fix it quick.

But there may be other priorities. There could be a new product or feature launch that you particularly want to keep abreast of; or there is a new regulatory requirement and you need to accelerate customer acknowledgement of their rights.

In Flow we are never prescriptive about how to plan priorities. It depends on the company and the environment. All we say is you need to make those priorities explicit, transparent and visual.

SIZING, EVALUATION AND VALUATION

This column on the Customer Feedback Wall serves two purposes. One needs to evaluate the impact of the customer pain point and, two, if possible assign a valuation for it. The evaluation allows you to allocate the pain point to 'no change required, or to 'a process change', or to a team for further analysis. The valuation drives the priority. For instance, can you put a $ number against a pain point? What is 'non-action' in this area costing you?

It is always worth having a stab at quantifying the cost question but it's often impossible to put an exact figure on it. You can maintain the tradition we talked about in Flow. Is it a $, $$ or $$$ problem? How long is it likely to take to resolve and what might its impact be on other parts of the service features or infrastructure?

You may also want to have a set of metrics to measure outputs from customer feedback. Don't opt for something as crude as the sheer number of amendments made. In talking with other Flow practitioners we have become acutely aware that old metrics of speed and throughput tell you little about quality. You need to seek out metrics like: an increase in inbound inquiries; a reduction in a particular complaint; recognition of process issues we had overlooked; more forms filled out to completion; extra sales on a particular product line.

NO CHANGE REQUIRED

Not all problems can be resolved by an action in a product team. If the complaint is price, you can send that kind of information upstairs to be evaluated but there is very little that can be done to resolve it without a change of strategy.

Increasingly, smart companies are choosing not to discount prices but instead to find gamified ways to incentivize customers to stay on the website and discover value. If there is a series of complaints about price, you may want to suggest gamification as a strategy for maintaining interaction with customers. But for now you have to say 'No Change Required'.

ASSIGNED TO DIGITAL TEAM

You will have your own terminology for this. Assigned to the digital team simply means that the complaint can be fixed by the team managing the company's online presence and sales channels. It is a local problem and can be fixed without impacting the platform.

ASSIGNED TO CORE TEAM

Sometimes it does need a change to the platform and in those cases it is assigned to a core team that has enough understanding of how to integrate changes with other areas of the platform architecture.

ASSIGNED TO PROCESS CHANGE

In some cases the customer complaint will be highlighting a fundamental flaw in your work processes (either online or in the back office). You may have a flurry of complaints around a feature set produced at more or less the same time, for example, that demonstrably have been poorly integrated.

Or it may be the user-logic has not been thought through adequately. For example imagine a situation whereby a customer is encouraged to apply for a product or associated feature, only to find out that they don't qualify because of age or some other disqualifying issue.

The process change in this case relates to getting customer qualifications earlier in the process. The change would simply be to say that people under X years or over Y years cannot apply for product Z upfront. Don't make them complete the entire customer journey only to be rejected. This time-waster will lose you a customer for life but it is surprising how often customer journeys are complete time-wasters.

In these cases it is not enough to provide a fix. You need to raise questions about how you work. Those questions go to the systems thinking group. They can also be aired at a Learning Wall and documented in the minimalist tradition of Flow. No drama, no blame. Just make sure you learn.

BACK TO THE PORTFOLIO WALL

A smaller class of customer feedback can also imply that errors have been made in strategic thinking. Say, executives have been too enthusiastic about a product-line. Or they've been slow to bury ideas that have been hanging out there for a long time with very little uptake. Whatever the reason might be, some features and products or even marketing ideas have to go back to be rethought.

In this case, they are projects. And they need to fight for priority on the Executive Portfolio Wall.

INFORMING CUSTOMERS

Finally there is the vitally important business of informing customers on your progress in responding to their concerns. Using regular communications to give them insights into your process and decisions will draw them closer to you.

CHAPTER 11

Broadening Your Personal Development Goals

Flow stands for empowerment. Real empowerment puts responsibilities onto your shoulders. It gives you more liberty, more uncertainty and more need to challenge yourself to grow. You define the change, after all. You are in charge of more than you realised.

This is in stark contrast to other frameworks. The Agile movement spawned a number of new tools and ways to work. Yet, the software platforms that grew up around Agile are major constraints on human talent. These include collaboration platforms like Atlassian's Jira and Confluence. Even though they are wildly successful, they distort people's views of assets and value.

Jira is a perfect fit for obsessive project managers who have turned to the scrum master role and like to keep order. Confluence is the surest way to bury information so nobody has to look at it again. They are heralded as collaboration tools but they are a way out of human interaction. They are document silos.

In place of these tools we need the Walls and conversations that we write about in Flow and that are flourishing as Kanban takes hold. People need more conversations about learning, improvement and personal development, real growth as opposed to databasing your brain for the corporation.

Here are three big reasons:

- As old roles break down and new ones emerge you need to be strong enough to set boundaries around yourself. That's not to say make yourself a silo. It is about being open but making your limits clear to other people, without being a jerk.

- In uncertain environments you need more emotional resilience. It is hard to set personal boundaries. People don't easily accept how you define your space and yet you need to do it with grace and calm. Emotional resilience is what helps you shape boundaries.

- You are going to have to be a quick study, learning new roles fast, learning people's strengths and weaknesses, adding in compassion and being a rounded person.

Traditionally, organisations have rarely perceived the value of emotional strength. They support braindumps of documents into Confluence when a better approach is to round out our skills so we can have the right intelligent conversations about value. To systematically improve value, you need to focus on the personal development goals of the people whose role is to create it.

THE IMPORTANCE OF PERSONAL DEVELOPMENT GOALS

In Flow we find people want to develop their capabilities. They seek out the opportunity to learn and frame their futures in a broader way than an organisation will. It is of value if people have improved communications as a goal. Mindfulness can be a goal. Value-seeking skills can be a goal.

In the example below a product owner has sought out her agile coach in order to develop her goals. This was not initiated by us but by two people who recognise the importance of personal development. A good learning agenda is defined by your people. It does not need to become a part of the HR conversation. People should interact around creating a very strong personal platform. The organisation benefits from that.

Arguably, the goals, below, do not go far enough. There's a growing school of thought that uncertainty is good for decision making and that not knowing is a positive. Viewed through the right lens, uncertainty can be motivating. We should not shy away from designing goals that make us more human, compassionate, doubtful and inquiring. Reading should broaden our horizons not just help us nail our jobs. Doubt, in fact, is power.

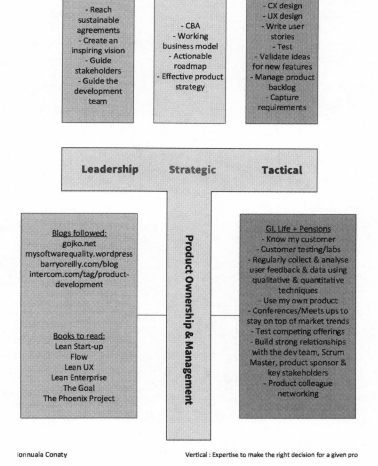

Horizontal : Ability to methodically solve common product challenges

- Reach sustainable agreements
- Create an inspiring vision
- Guide stakeholders
- Guide the development team

- CBA
- Working business model
- Actionable roadmap
- Effective product strategy

- SQL
- CX design
- UX design
- Write user stories
- Test
- Validate ideas for new features
- Manage product backlog
- Capture requirements

Leadership   Strategic   Tactical

Blogs followed:
gojko.net
mysoftwarequality.wordpress
barryoreilly.com/blog
intercom.com/tag/product-development

Books to read:
Lean Start-up
Flow
Lean UX
Lean Enterprise
The Goal
The Phoenix Project

Product Ownership & Management

GI, Life + Pensions
- Know my customer
- Customer testing/labs
- Regularly collect & analyse user feedback & data using qualitative & quantitative techniques
- Use my own product
- Conferences/Meets ups to stay on top of market trends
- Test competing offerings
- Build strong relationships with the dev team, Scrum Master, product sponsor & key stakeholders
- Product colleague networking

Ion nuala Conaty   Vertical : Expertise to make the right decision for a given pro

CAUGHT NOT TAUGHT: THE ART OF CONTINUOUS LEARNING

Continuous learning needs to be guided by this broader range of personal goals. Much of what you will learn in a Flow environment comes right out of the conversations and debates going on between peers. You need a strong personal platform in order to make sense of it, systematically.

An Agile coach we work with put it better than we can: Flow is caught not taught. In other words you capture what you can from the intense social interaction in a good workplace. You don't sit down in a two day coaching session and hope to come out with a qualification that makes you a winner. The fact that we are able to capture some portion of what flows around us but not all of it, is really the source of group power. This is why we are together.

That in fact is the real meaning of collective intelligence - shaping the flow of knowledge together. This wonderful surge of human activity not only means your workplace is changing. It also means that you, the person willing to learn, are at the heart of it. You are the change.

In the remainder of this chapter we are going to relate those principles to five issues:

1. How your organisation, wrongly, expects you to learn.

2. How to develop your personal learning objectives.

3. Thinking about your learning style (where we will touch on our own personal learning styles).

4. How roles are changing in work.

5. And developing a personal learning journal.

If you want to go straight to the How-to jump to point 5 now.

1. AGAINST TRADITIONAL ORGANISATIONAL LEARNING

You face a contradiction. Organisations want you to be creative but also to learn "the organisation's way". Our colleague Dan Pontefract put this very succinctly. All your school-life you are taught the value of thinking freely. Then you go to work!

Firms have a right to expect some conformity. But mostly they over-regulate behaviour. Your value lies in how well you develop yourself not in how willing you are to obey rules.

Dan is right about another point. People in work need a purpose. We believe the purpose is to seek value. This simple realisation drives us to learn continuously and to improve the flow of work day after day. Once the flow is improved, everything passing through it benefits. But it begins with you, your interactions and the search for value.

Along with your colleagues you will face the need to come up with totally new solutions. As well as being a smart person, you need the skills that allow you to participate in designing new ways to work.

Organisational learning fits you out with the skills it takes to function in a process-driven framework. We've said from the start that we are process-lite. Flow is the minimalist framework for business agility. We don't want all the rules that go with an old process bound by rules. Good process is something that smart people create in the flow and then change when appropriate.

However, most corporate training, and this includes Agile, is centred on specific process objectives and their metrics. We are against this type of learning. It forces people to commit to a mind-set that rejects new ideas. Plus learning is a personal obligation. If you cannot be bothered to stretch yourself intellectually, you don't belong in a Flow team.

2. DEVELOPING YOUR PERSONAL LEARNING OBJECTIVES

Living with uncertainty means setting appropriate boundaries so that you have a strong inner core; and growing your emotional resilience so that uncertainty becomes empowering. Paradoxical but true. You can prosper with uncertainty. If you have a better sense of yourself and you can project that, everything will work out better.

In a continuous learning environment you face the problem of continuously feeling you don't quite know enough. Congratulations! You just spotted your most intelligent and powerful attribute. People become unnecessarily anxious in that position. They may have to speak about a topic they haven't mastered or be encouraged to do a stand-up before they are ready. It becomes a source of anxiety that works against them. Turn it round. Uncertainty gives you the opportunity to grow, invent and be smarter. It is a source of power.

You cannot avoid exposing what you don't know. In order to do this successfully you need to embrace the limits we all face.

Here's an example. Haydn often has to talk about changes in global geopolitics. In key respects this is an unknowable area. Anything can happen to disrupt what appear to be established patterns of activity. However, a clue lies in that very idea. Are there really so many patterns in the activity you see around you? Or are we really only ever able to take a snapshot these days? Is it smart to pretend we know where things are at? Or smarter to nail the doubts up for people to see? Doubt provides you with an opportunity to be creative and to share a journey.

Today, you cannot have confidence that any pattern of activity will last. Your confidence lies in the fact that disruption will happen sooner rather than later. Having confidence in your sense of uncertainty comes down to dividing these realities clearly in your mind. We need to take a degree of pride in not knowing. In the age of uncertainty, you need learning objectives that can define a creative future for you.

Here are some of our (Haydn and Fin's) learning objectives.

- ***Making a difference with a new movement.*** We seek knowledge because of our life goals - being able to make a difference, whether that's helping one other person to change or helping an organisation, we want people to enjoy learning. For us Flow is a movement. It is not our movement. Flow is a philosophy of personal and group empowerment through better social interaction. Flow is about your power and our power and how we grow it.

- ***Continuous personal growth***: Both of us want to grow on a daily basis. We hope we rarely end the day knowing the same as we did at the beginning. In Ireland, when people are confronted with bad experiences, they often say: Well, at least I learned. That's pretty much how we think. If we do nothing else, each day we can learn.

- ***Being a peer:*** We're both able and willing to call out bullshit. There's too much of it around. It can be some of the most respected management theories or it can be widely used software platforms or popular influencers. They are not always helpful but people swarm around them. For us, all good work comes down to the quality of interaction between people. You don't need more of a theory than that.

- ***Durability and resilience:*** It is popular in the mobile, social media world to believe that change can be continuous and yet is somehow trivial. Our friend Bill Johnston is one of the world's leading authorities in community management. Bill has grown with community management, never deviating from his belief that work is about communities rather than hierarchies. Peers like this inspire us to stick with stuff even when it feels nobody else is listening.

- *Knowing the detail:* We are interested in the detail of what's going on around us. In Fin's case, as a leader he can't possibly know all the detail but he can be broadly enough based in his learning that he can give permission for the right things to happen. In fact it is a hallmark of his leadership. Fin is one of the great permission givers. Haydn is more likely to get involved in long iterative knowledge projects. For example he has been working on understanding human ecosystems for about a decade now. You can be broad and you can be detailed at the same time.

- *Vision:* Vision, for us, comes with a small "v". We both have a vision of how things can be different, particularly in the creation of a much more social and enjoyable work environment that is less rigid and less structured. In Fin's case the vision is also shaped by his belief that good outcomes can be shaped by applying common sense. Common sense know-how is a seam of gold waiting to be mined but very often leaders are too grand or lofty to see it.

- *Spiritual gains:* Fin runs multiple marathons each year as a way of setting and meeting personal goals to stretch his physical capabilities and achieve spiritual gains like calmness and detachment. Haydn hikes around some of Europe's most beautiful mountain ranges for the same reasons. Work puts us under so much pressure that these spiritual journeys help recharge us. Ideas pop out when you are on the 30th kilometre of a race or taking a breather at 10,000 feet. The most amazingly clear fact is that finally our society is changing for the better and more people are empowered to define work for themselves.

We pointed out in Chapter 6 that all the thinking, learning and interacting is in pursuit of value. We want to create value because we want to be valued.

3. THINKING ABOUT YOUR LEARNING STYLE

So as much as we have emphasised your personal learning goals so far, the overall objective is value. But what about techniques? Like all CIOs Fin is pretty busy but he also builds in time for a number of formal learning opportunities. Here's his short list:

Fin's learning style:

1. Podcasts

I listen to everything from Amazon Web Services' podcasts to shows about Life Hacking and Exponential Innovation. Admittedly it takes time to find a rich vein of gold but believe me it's there.

2. Meetup.com

This is a great source of free events run by and attended by enthusiasts in certain topics. My meetups range from DevOps, UX Design, Big Data and Alexa Development to Blockchain.

3. Thinking time

Running, walking and swimming are great opportunities to exercise the grey matter. I know that Haydn enjoys these types of activities, as do I, and I get some of my greatest ideas when just walking to the office.

4. LinkedIn, Twitter etc

In amongst a lot of irrelevant information, I get great nuggets of interesting topics. But sometimes you have to work hard to find them!

5. Standups

In my company we run standups across a range of domain groups including executive standups, formal agile standups and learning standups. I always learn from colleagues at these.

6. Conferences

I try not just to attend conferences but also to speak at them. Apart from the buzz and a little bit of ego massaging (!) speaking forces you to do homework. You have to revise and structure your thoughts. It represents a kind of learning milestone.

7. *Debriefs*

However, improving the Flow is not always about adding new stuff. It is crucial to reflect at all stages of the framework and learn.

In our first book, we talk about retrospectives and the different methods that are used to reflect together. This is a great way of learning and self-improvement. But I've been trying to increase the opportunities for reflection in order to learn more "in the moment" and hence gain more improvement. I recently came across a technique used by the Red Arrows Aerobatic Team which they use after every flight. The *Debrief.*

Simply put, you can use this after every meeting, every event and every stage of a project. Everyone on the team has the opportunity to say what we should Stop, Start or Continue doing. Even a small improvement to a humble regular meeting fuels the aggregation of marginal gains/improvements.

LEARNING WALLS

Learning Walls are a way to process these different techniques and to get some kind of rough consensus on what we are learning as a group (see Flow for more).

HAYDN'S LEARNING STYLE

I have quite a different learning style from Fin. Mine is much less social. Fin is always in the mix, always available to people or "managing up". A lot of what he achieves happens through those social relationships day-to-day.

Having said our styles differ, however, I do find that my learning style changes periodically. I hope that's a good guideline for you. How you learn has to change over time. Five years ago I was intense about reading diligently on the topics I advised people about. I wanted to have the detail pinned down before I wrote or spoke. My learning style was very archive based.

At other times it needed to be based on interviews with people in the know. I might be thinking about AI and realise the only way to take a view is to interview 30 people who are using AI (or not). In effect I try to aggregate the state of knowledge and then offer some insights. And that's a pretty good guideline for some companies to follow. Seek out multiple experts: synthesise and discuss.

Today it is different because much of my work, like yours, is devoted to figuring out how to do things that have not yet been done. I can't do this if I only rely on research or interviews. I need a way to think and iterate that doesn't depend on the opinions of others until I'm ready. A bit like a chef, I want to cook something up and then share it, and ask if the mix is inspiring or not.

On the desk in my office are two hundred A3 sheets of paper. This personal visualisation space has a very specific objective. Like Fin, I increasingly work visually but it would be hopeless for me to be asking for feedback or posing ideas to my peers when the ideas are not sufficiently thought through (though I have made the mistake of going public too early often enough!).

I try to sketch out a problem and its solution every day. I mean every day. It's rare that a day goes by when I don't try to visualise a problem and try to draw an answer. My pages are an attempt to draw out a complete world so that I can see all the elements. To take a real example, the problem might be: How do you structure a business ecosystem so that environmental depletion is not an inevitable consequence of modern industrial supply chains?

In other words global supply is often very damaging, even though we are encouraged to laud global trade. The "cost" is often externalised, i.e. a penalty we all have to pay, such as global warm-

ing, in exchange for a cheap product, such as cut flowers. I start to
think about issues like this by sketching:

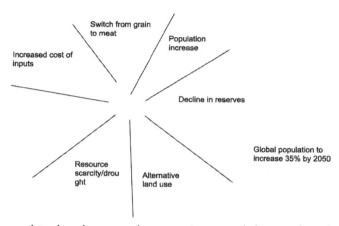

I gave this sketch to my designer Anna and this is what she came
back with, below. When I look at her design I already know I am
wrong. My diagram lacks something I can't put my finger on. The
iteration has, however, helped me to dig deeper.

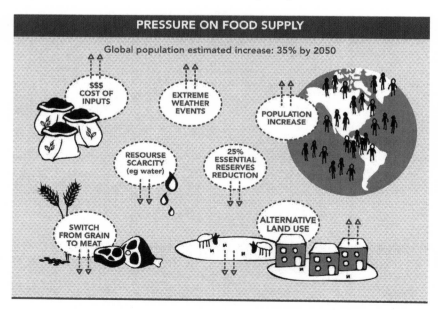

Because supply chains are so complex, locating solutions to the problem of environmental depletion is just plain difficult, unless you can see it drawn out in front of you. Drawing it out throws up a new problem area: What are the appropriate incentives for creating good environmental behaviour and outcomes? How can these be organised?

These thoughts provoke questions about the staging and timing of solutions. These initial sketches were in fact part of a larger project to build a blockchain and cryptocurrency solution for food supply. After Anna had done her work I was able to add in some thoughts about how a currency might work and where incentives would be needed. But without the help of someone who sees things more literally than I do (I am trapped in words), I find it difficult to move my thinking on. Collaboration with visual thinkers is essential to me.

I work these ideas through before I go to colleagues with my thoughts. My learning style is just that: Draw - iterate - explore consequences - consult peers - iterate.

Here's another visual example. This was me sketching out how Flow might be structured as a learning project. What are the key elements from the 200 page book and the 12 steps:

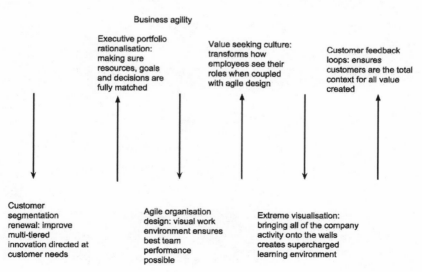

Business agility

Executive portfolio rationalisation: making sure resources, goals and decisions are fully matched

Value seeking culture: transforms how employees see their roles when coupled with agile design

Customer feedback loops: ensures customers are the total context for all value created

Customer segmentation renewal: improve multi-tiered innovation directed at customer needs

Agile organisation design: visual work environment ensures best team performance possible

Extreme visualisation: bringing all of the company activity onto the walls creates supercharged learning environment

Here's what Anna made of my sketch:

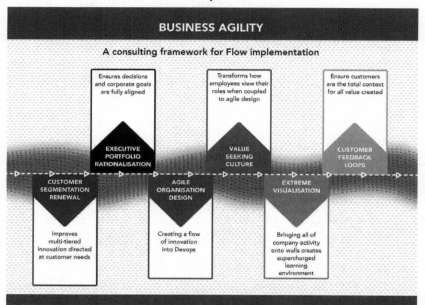

This still isn't a finished framework. At this stage it is something I can share with someone, in this case Fin. What I'm showing him also shows I am invested in this line of thinking, so he is more likely to respect it and engage,

Fin and I work differently but we have one thing in common. We both want to find new ways to work that are really empowering. There's a place to start that in a personal learning journal (see point 5).

4. TEN EVOLVING ROLES IN WORK

To set your learning objectives you need to know how roles are changing. And you need to know how to design work!

There are very specific new roles in domains like Big Data. You need people, for example, who know about data normalisation or analytics. But did you know that the lead at the AI program at American Express actually trained as a historian? Yes, and the reason why? Because AI needs forensic brains, people who are prepared to keep coming back to a problem and learning more about how to flesh out the solution, week after week. These are people who know the story is never fully written.

Here's a few observations on the changing roles in organisations.

The initiator. We know of some great minds who continually get projects underway. They pull in the resources and fire up enthusiasm levels and get people ready to haul the wagon-train to a new destination. These people may not have the staying power or skills to manage a project long-term but without them, projects stay in committees and pipelines for an age. The initiator often has an insatiable need to know and to be on the edge.

The wrangler. Some of the early Flow projects, and Flow techniques, were shaped by people who were just damn good at never letting go of a problem. Asked to produce a new platform in a ridiculously short space of time, they batted off each other for three months to create a flow of work that would deliver in an impossible time frame.

A. They are so dogged in the quest to learn that they never let go of a problem until there is resolution.

B. They can take the rejection and occasional ridicule that goes with proposing answers non-stop; they are driven by ambiguity.

C. They know not to use any one example as the exemplary case; like a test batsman who has scored a hundred, they know when to scratch out their mark again and start over as if they hadn't a single run to their name.

The connector. Projects get greenlit because of this person's political skills and capacity to manage other people's objectives. They marry people and ideas together. To do that successfully they have fine empathetic skills. And they are helped along with some formal psychological knowledge of how people's behaviour reflects their underlying goals.

The coach. There are thousands of people out there carrying around a badge called Agile Coach. For the most part they are believers in some of the most valuable ideas to touch the business world, those captured in the Agile Manifesto. Trouble is the work practices are outdated. Agile coaches know their work needs to change and they are hungry for new ideas. They want to break down rigid processes and replace them with invention and interaction. They need to get comfortable with invention on-the-fly.

The product or project guy. Very few people know how to take a blank sheet of paper and grow a project or a product from that empty space. To do that you need to be able to iterate ideas from early beginnings into loosely described plans that give just enough detail to get people enthusiastic about taking on new roles. They have economic, market and technical know-how but above all else that elusive skill of being able to define something that does not exist. They got there by participating, by taking on creative projects, by experiencing the evolution of creative ideas.

The mediator. The work environment is becoming potentially conflict full. In the past we've been able to sit out conflicts, leave badass people alone, and plough our own furrow. It won't work anymore. We have to be able to confront behaviour that gets in the way of value. Groups work better when there is a good share of voice. But even then there needs to be people with good mediation skills allied to a level of knowledge and experience that earns respect for a conciliatory voice.

The tester. All business at some stage becomes about a test or a metric. You've heard people say, if you cannot measure it, you can't execute. This turns out to be wrong. You can test and measure close to your instincts. Flow often leads people to abandon formal reports and to rely instead on photographs of Walls. Testing becomes less of a formal framework and more a matter or smart people getting together and asking: Is this ready to go in front of a few customers? Having people in the test and measurement area who are ready take the formality away is a big advantage.

The detective. Teams need that forensic mind we referred to earlier. Many big projects are now broken down into multiple small projects. That's true of IT in general - microservices leads to hundreds of separate software projects and packages all communicating with each other. It is also true of marketing. Unilever's Foundry invites dozens of startups to interact with its business units in search of new ways to get product to market. Small leads to a new kind of complexity and having some folks on hand who are delighted by the forensic detail without getting too pedantic, is a must.

The tech guru. You want technical mastery of your area, even if you are in marketing. You want to be the person that can be a source of value to your peers through your knowledge of technique, platforms, functionality. Plenty of people in open source projects take that road.

The emotional leader. In the book Flow we make a big point of underlining a leader's need to learn rather than to demonstrate superior know-how. Being visible about learning is important and you can read more in Flow. But the bigger point we make is to find leaders who care about people's emotions and won't cop out by saying *it's just business*.

We hope you can see from this short list that a lot of what firms and teams need are people who are forging a distinct character and skill set through their willingness to learn continuously. They are prepared to risk looking foolish in order to advance an idea but they hope to have peers who know how chancy and hard it can be to raise your hand and take a guess at how to solve a new problem. They are more deeply social than people have been over the past 30 years or more in work. They can't be contained by a silo. They want to initiate, wrangle, connect and lead.

5. A PERSONAL LEARNING WALL

Part of this journey needs to be a clear idea of the type of person you are, which of these new roles has the strongest appeal and your ability to map out a road to success. It is worth developing these elements in a mindful way. What might a personal learning journal look like and what questions might help you build it? Why not try a Wall. Add a Done row to the Wall below as you progress your personal goals.

A Personal Development Wall

GOALS ⟶

GOALS	Work specific skills	Relationship skills	Emotional	Spiritual
Short term	▢ ▢ ◼	▢ ▢	▢ ▢	▢ ▢
Long term	▢ ▢	▢	▢	◼ ▢

◼ Big issue   ▢ Medium   ▢ Small

These Post-Its could include things like:

- Improving specific technical skills.
- Learning how to mediate.

- Taking mindfulness courses.

- Joining a public speaking course.

- Understanding the value of being introvert.

- Building a stronger sense of self.

- Learning how to deal with aggression.

- Exploring uncertainty as a power advantage.

- Reading about Not Knowing.

- Taking a team psychology qualification.

There is no point in us listing more because we think you get the point. Your personal development will propel your professional development. Here's some questions you might ask:

1. A definition of your short and long term term career goals but also your social objectives.

    a. Short term, what role do you want to play in a team? Think carefully about this because you are going to craft your role and style over a long period of time. Commit it to your A3 or Wall. Do you have a tendency to jump in when other people are talking? Can you prepare for a culture where opinions get more respect? Can you shape equal share of voice? Can you guide and facilitate other people? Are you a mediator? Or a tech expert?

    b. Long term, how would you like your continuing education to define you and your position in a company? Work will continue to change and it will become more social and more interactive so you are going to need more soft skills and relationship skills. Who do you envision when you look ahead? Imagine what authority will you have and how will you carry that authority. What kind of leader will you be in teams that need plenty of leaders?

c. What will your role be as a peer? Can you commit to a personal development path that makes you more active in meetings, more confident in presentations, more able to lead in a supportive way? Or are you going to be the wrangler-type whose real passion is "the problem"?

2. A set of learning objectives as we have described above:

a. The specific personal characteristics that fit you for a role in a Flow environment are qualities like the ability to be at ease with uncertainty; a willingness to interact frequently over difficult problems and stay calm; the ability to sketch things out on a wall along with colleagues and in real time move your thinking forward. It takes practice. Your gold dust is out in front of people but so too is your naivety. You should also think in terms of durability and tenacity, and a lack of intransigence, not just with your career path but also with the detail of work. Do you have an ability to imagine the downstream consequences of decisions? You might need to become good at options thinking or figuring out the potential second order consequences of any decision.

b. How can you fit yourself out to be a strong person in an iterative and often experimental environment full of uncertainty? Fin and Haydn both strive to be the person who never let's personal bias and prejudice get in the way of a professional judgment. You have to learn about your biases (there's a string of articles on different bias characteristics you can consult). We want to be the people who can diffuse tension when passions run high, as they should from time to time.

You develop these traits intentionally by observing the people around you and understanding that they are playing to their strengths and displaying their weaknesses. Talk to counsellors and psychologists to find out specifically what you need to learn to function well. One thing really worth understanding is that most people seek affirmation. A lot of the affirmation on offer in organisations is phoney but good leaders create work processes that lead to real gains for people.

c.   Generate and record insights into your learning style and reflect on what you find problematic. Reflect too on what you find enjoyable about going into work. People learn through interaction (so don't immediately push back on views that seem alien to yours); give people's ideas space to grow; they learn visually (shape a conversation by saying - can we sketch that out?); they learn by reading (Aviva now has a Flow community that includes a reading circle that stretches people with what they should read); people learn through rejection (make it safe to get push back/make it fun!); people learn by catching onto what's happening (use Walls to capture learning).

3.   A daily learning objective, to be sure you progress continuously.

    a.   A practical objective such as leading instead of following or attending a meetup or Flow Circle with a determination to make a contribution.

    b.   An abstract objective that lets you get out of the routine you are in to let new ideas flow.

    c.   A creative objective such as photography or writing that teaches you about how to test and iterate ideas in a safe environment. As an example, Haydn is a terrible flower photographer but he has given himself ten years to learn how to be the best! Using your spare time to test creative hypotheses is just part of living a full life. And it helps with work.

YOU ARE THE VALUE

It is up to you to define your learning objectives and find your learning style. You need to be aware that the chances are very high that your requirements are going to include invention of some kind. So you need to think how roles are changing, what roles you are suited to and how you will cope with being the inventor of a new process, a new feature or model for how a particular area of work gets done.

Once you discover something new as a team, you are "permitted" to add it to Flow. There's no governing body to impress or papers to write. Plug it in, reap the rewards and start gaining the value.

CHAPTER 12

Small Steps to an Agile Strategy

The final step in becoming a good Flow workplace is to challenge the idea of big strategy and grand plans. The new method is to build strategy up from small steps. In this chapter we are going to look at how that can be achieved. We'll go through a simple exercise to look at how big strategy can evolve through small actions.

We will look at business platform strategy. Business platforms are one of the most exciting areas of the economy (think Alibaba, Transferwise, Airbnb, and Apple's App Store). They control multiple strands of economic activity: room renting, car rides, smartphone apps, social networks, music, games etc. They generally achieve a dominant position in their markets so what's not to love.

The problem in trying to build a business platform is that the core elements, the ones people focus on in strategy and planning, are necessary but nowhere near sufficient for success.

The necessary-but-not-sufficient problem is typical of the digital world. Many additional factors, often intangibles like online relationships, play a significant role in scaling up digital businesses. The intangible nature of these inputs is very difficult for traditional strategists to grasp. They focus on what is *necessary from an older business perspective*. They are driven by the cold, hard facts, as they see them. Build the platform and market the hell out of it. They tend also to be advised by IT, who see the platform as a technology stack not a relationship nexus.

There are big knowledge gaps in how people think about Platforms. We will illustrate how to overcome those challenges one step at a time.

Why is this so interesting to Flow? First, Platforms invented modern agility. They set the benchmark for transformation and they demonstrate that the journey is not just about process change. Platforms are masters at moving into new markets (are you using Apple Pay, Google Pay, Samsung Pay? Then you are experiencing the power of technology platforms to roam into any space they choose). A lot of their activity takes place on the network and can be updated with high frequency at low cost. Feedback loops from users give decision makers constant access to market insights. Products are digital too, which means there is no conventional supply chain to manage.

Second, Platforms are almost impossible to plan. Execution needs a huge amount of iteration and a commitment to real-time executive direction. Much of the investment carries risks that are difficult to anticipate and then mitigate. Those risks might be: the need to attract third parties to, say, build apps, provide data or provide content. Nobody can say what it will cost to be successful at developing the ecosystem of third party actors.

Platforms force their designers to take small steps. From an operational point of view they force their owners to take many hundreds of incremental steps and this requires Flow. Incremental steps are good. Some of the greatest examples of human achievement stem from the many small steps approach rather than the design of any single large initiative. The idea of incrementalism is in fact very common. It permeates all sectors of achievement.

One of Picasso's most famous works, Guernica, is actually made up of characters that he had used in previous works. At times the painting was far more emotive than the finished product. Early on, he included a clenched fist in his sketches. At one stage he used colour. All these elements were stripped away before completion. In other words, he composed this vast symbol of mindless cruelty in warfare in many small steps that were switched in and out to get to the point of being done.

We often convey the impression in business that there is one big solution (a new platform) or a single answer to complex problems. This is just wrong. When leaders proudly boast that we should simplify, they deny us access to the advantages of introspection and careful, stepwise progress.

SUCCESS IN HIGH PERFORMANCE TEAMS

In delivery terms, the economy is shifting towards small. That includes the growing importance of small companies to large enterprises; the shift to small software packages in microservices architectures; the growth of micro-outsourcing; and of course enterprise ecosystems.

Good leaders recognise that critical gains lie in the margins, in the detail. That's why in Flow, work units are only ever a maximum of 2 days long. These are the micro-units where you can get the 1% gains to scale up into something significant.

Incremental can sound dull. We are in the age of exponential growth, after all. However, hundreds of small increments of change per day are precisely what large enterprises need. Incremental change at scale can apply to strategy and it can apply to delivery. increasingly it will become the way enterprises achieve excellence.

Breaking work down into 2 day cycles means people have to interact more, which is also good for productivity and quality. And it plays into the visualisation of work. The only way to manage the flow properly is if it is visible. Two day cycles keep work out in the open.

Shorter cycle-times are good also because they allow teams to pivot. More than that they allow teams to get rid of project work quickly when it is irrelevant to customer value.

We argue that you stand a far better chance of getting to a new kind of Pareto Efficiency (the point where work is so optimised that any further changes reduce efficiency somewhere else) with small steps. Teams will improve processes that they codesign to meet the needs of small tasks. Teams struggle to codesign large projects and large processes. Inevitably these are given over to people who specialise in planning. That private planning project will rarely be greeted with an improving ethos among employees. They will execute. They may execute well or badly. But they are unlikely to improve the process.

SMALL STEPS TO A BIG PLATFORM

One problem with setting digital strategy is that many people get the core ideas of agility and scale wrong. A consensus has formed too quickly around key terms. In the agile world, where digital transformation dominates our thinking, companies seek network effects, for example. Their aim is to become a platform business like an Airbnb or an Uber. At the very least, they want to avoid being disrupted by these platforms. There is something uniquely powerful about them, supposedly created through:

- Open APIs (the practice of providing a software doorway to an asset like data or functionality).

- Two sided or multi-sided markets.

- Network effects.

- Cloud infrastructure.

These are the supposedly necessary components. But the formula is very flawed and we need to rework popular opinion for the sake of absolute clarity.

1. First of all, great platforms exist without having an open API (Airbnb, Netflix). The open API cannot even be said to be necessary, let alone sufficient for greatness.

2. Second, the idea of two-sided and multi-sided markets feels superfluous. Yes, markets can be a good way of organising supply and purchasing. They do represent a shift in how enterprises function, endowing one company with utility-like power as the market organiser. But the insights for strategy are low-level. If you look closely at platforms, you see that very often there are members of the ecosystem who simply do not touch the platform infrastructure. They are the companies that are providing marginal gains to the platform world without actually being a supplier into or a buyer out of a market. They have a marginal impact rather than a necessary one. They are part of the critical non-essentials.

3. Third, network effects are powerful but rare. Facebook has network effects. In order for me to enjoy Facebook, I need my network to use it too. I become more than an advocate. I am a recruiter and so too will all my network members be. However, most of us cannot access this viral power. We do not enjoy network effects. We enjoy the effect of being on a network. There's a big difference. Sadly for platform theory we all have access to the benefits of networks.

4.   Similarly with Cloud services. There's nothing special about
      that. All companies have access to Cloud infrastructure.

The real power of platforms, the sufficient part, lies in the
ecosystems that grow around the successful ones. Now, isn't that
a tenuous formula! The ecosystem is often made up of the third
party companies that form around platforms and turn them into
something special. But the ecosystem doesn't truly form until entrepreneurs begin to see, or strongly anticipate, success.

This is a nightmare for traditional strategists. It means success
lies at the other end of intangible investments in relationships,
promotion, content, and likeability.

Here is a very good example from among dozens we could
have chosen. On Amazon's market platforms there are a number of
services that owe no allegiance to Amazon but who have spotted an
opportunity to optimise the Amazon service. One of them is book
arbitrage or search arbitrage.

There are dozens of companies on Amazon that specialise in
discovering cheap books on the platform, buying these, and then
reselling them at a much higher price on the same platform. The
arbitrage skill lies in knowing Amazon's search engine and paid
marketing services well enough that through arbitrage a customer
is able to find a book that was previously hidden well down the
Amazon search returns pages.

Think about this for a second. The impact of an arbitrage service
is that the customer pays a lot more for what she buys. The upside is
she finds it. She enjoys success.

These companies are an essential part of the Amazon ecosystem
but their arrival was not prompted, supported by or invested in by
Amazon. In fact they exist because of Amazon's shortcomings. The
Amazon deficit sparked an entrepreneurial opportunity. Similarly,

there are now dozens of cleaning services and remote access providers that allow Airbnb to function as well as it does. These services do not even touch the Airbnb platform.

The "sufficient" part of strategy, the critical non-essentials, is capricious. Strategy has to involve investments that allow intangibles and unseen opportunities to emerge.

THE VERY BASIC MODEL FOR HIGHLY SCALED BUSINESS

Platforms do have a basic structure that is necessary without being sufficient. There are elements that can be planned and these tempt strategists to believe that the necessary encompasses the sufficient. It blinds them to the critical non-essentials.

In essence, most platforms come down to a few basic components, though these are by no means always present:

The basic format for a platform business

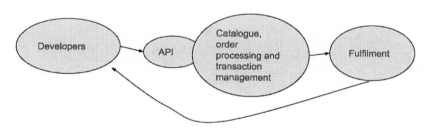

A company opens up APIS to data, to functionality or a catalogue. The owners hope this access will attract developers to create apps or services that expand the platform owner's market. That's more or less what happened with the App Store and the iPhone.

Many platforms are indeed a basic ordering platform. They are a catalogue with a transaction engine and fulfilment service. Even Airbnb fits that description. It is a catalogue of rooms, apartments and houses. It has an ordering system and a transaction engine to allow customers to pay for an order. The host then fulfils the order by welcoming guests.

The simplicity, however, is misleading. It is true that all the elements in the model are important. But they are easy to acquire. What sits on top of the platform and all around it are highly scaled relationships, many giveaway tools, wonderful content and huge advocacy.

Many firms fail to appreciate how all these other components contribute to success. They have the simple model in mind. They create the plan: build a software development kit; create developer guidelines; open the API; create the transaction process; and tie this into a fulfilment network (such as room renters or car drivers). Then they wait for network effects to kick in. In fast growing markets (such as bike rentals) it can work for a while but the lack of real relationships will ultimately bite back.

Many companies create platforms without realising that content and advocacy are key aspects of the project. Content and advocacy rely on human factors, a truth that platform designers overlook. And they are difficult to represent in an ROI plan. Traditionalists looking at line items covering content and advocacy would ask: can't we cut that? Businesses are accustomed to look for savings in every plan they create. They jump on cost not value.

In addition, the activities that go with recruiting and nurturing relationships are not easily planned. They require warmth, trust, care, excitement and adaptability. Their cost/return is always going to be uncertain. And because businesses have been taught to expect network effects, they underinvest in advocacy, the very thing that could bring the benefits of being on a network.

We say *unfortunately* because being on a network is only powerful if you know how to acquire great content and generate superb advocacy. People must love what you are doing madly enough to create content around it, build new services to exploit it, recommend features of your service that they will attach their reputations to, and spend their own cash on being part of your ecosystem.

THE IMPORTANCE OF THE ECOSYSTEM

The attraction and orchestration of multiple parties to a passionate endeavour are difficult skills to acquire. That's why we say so much strategy these days is really about small steps. A Flow approach to strategy aims at creating the dozens of small steps that allow entrepreneurs or executives to figure out where value might lie and to accelerate business activity in precisely those directions. To do Flow strategy, you have to accept that you cannot know. You can hypothesise frequently across many actions and be ready to find out some basic truths you can build on.

This is far from the idea of an MVP. Many platforms don't need an MVP. They need the minimum sustainable delivery matrix we talked about earlier. They need a broad set of features and hypotheses to push through to customers. And they need structured feedback loops to capture knowledge. That knowledge has to be captured in formats that are easily translated into discussions that lead to new feature and hypothesis matrices.

One of the techniques we use to unblock thinking in platform strategy is the asset discovery process, described in Chapter 2. You might remember the diagram below from way back. It shows the relationship between customer segmentation, exploring unmet needs, asset identification, innovation ideas and ecosystems. We will explore those features in a little more detail now.

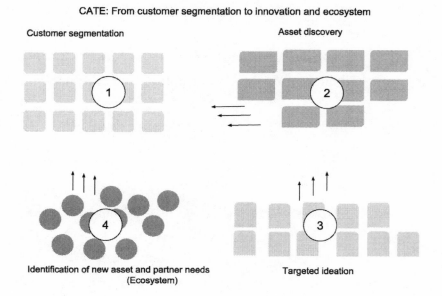

CUSTOMER SEGMENTATION

CUSTOMER SEGMENTATION

New digital platforms have two interesting characteristics. The first is they take on the challenge of reorganising a market (room rentals, freelance labour, currency exchange and remittance, media distribution). The second is that by doing this, they have an unparalleled opportunity to make segmentation part of their feedback loops.

For example Netflix only needed to know that people were willing to stream media into their homes in order to gradually build a complex segmentation based on the genres people tend to watch.

Equally Airbnb can enjoy a segmentation based on where people go to and what property types they choose, now supplemented with experiences. We'll go with the flow on this one and assume that the strategy we are about to explore is based on a segment that the platform advocate knows to be under-served or in need of reorganisation.

ASSET DISCOVERY

Any business strategy is really about how to grow, deploy and exploit assets that meet needs. Value generally originates in exploiting underused assets. In the new economy, companies typically try to exploit third party assets. That's almost the definition of a business platform.

Of course Platforms have their own assets (the transaction engine, for example). They may have assets they didn't realise they had (new brand perceptions or new tools that are unexploited). They are familiar with Cloud but can get stalled on a decision while waiting for a C-Suite policy. But generally speaking, putting aside these issues, they need to go in search of other assets. These can be assets they can orchestrate in a marketplace (seats in cars, rooms, developer talent, content, data). Or they can be those critical non-essentials (arbitrage services, third party content and tools, access providers and so on).

In a platform economy many companies fail to think through the orchestration of a broad ecosystem of partners, non-partner third parties and critical non-essential elements like content. They wait for network effects to kick in. And they wait some more.

Articulating small steps to a big strategy

KNOWN PLATFORM ASSETS
SDK
TRANSACTION ENGINE
SOME CONTENT
LOGISTICS
CLOUD
MIGRATION

MISSING ASSETS
END-CONSUMER SEGMENTATION / LONG TAIL DYNAMICS
RECOMMENDATION ENGINE
SOCIAL TOOLS
END-USER CONTENT
MORE CREATIVE TOOLS
ENGAGING DEV CONTENT
FLEXIBILITY IN SDK
ECOSYSTEM DYNAMICS
ADVOCACY

UNRECOGNISED ASSETS
CREATIVE TOOLS
RELATIONSHIP STRENGTHS
BRAND FACTORS
LOCAL CULTURE

The diagram above is an account of assets that are easy to acquire or create (known assets); assets that are hidden in the organisation and assets that need to be developed (missing assets). It is not an exhaustive list but it is a start for anyone wanting to think through a strategy.

Known platform assets: In the first bubble, top left, we have listed out assets that are present in the simple model of a platform.

Companies underestimate what it takes to create even these "simple" platform assets. It is not unusual for companies, even in the ecommerce space, to have poor transaction engines (lacking popular payment options, for example, or being too costly for small payments); or for their finance departments to be extremely reluctant to deal with micropayments.

The Cloud Migration issue presents a similar challenge. Strategists know they have to grow their platform in the Cloud but are prone to interpret that big policy decision as a big technical project. In fact, it can be done easily and cheaply in small steps that are all aimed at creating incremental value. However, just as Large Corp has too long a cadence of work, it also wants big projects! Cloud becomes a complex issue for no better reason than big companies complicate their decisions.

Even these known assets therefore need bolstering as part of the small steps approach.

Unknown platform and ecosystem assets. In the lower left bubble there are unrecognised or unknown assets. These emerge once a company begins to think in a fresh way about its techniques, image and strengths. It will find that some part of its operations have already created tools that are not widely used but could be repurposed for an ecosystem. The tools might be, say, accounting modules that could be converted into a support tool for ecosystem members. A new perception of the brand could easily be developed or there could be an easily exploited relationship that is currently ignored. Companies need to explore their assets especially as they are broadening their customer segmentation.

Missing assets: On the right are missing assets. Good customer segmentation is an asset missing from many strategy playbooks. The tools that allow you to access the long-tail are also important (that's why arbitrage works on Amazon). Companies operating online often have to develop tools to give to the ecosystem. Think of Google's Analytics tools, a first class critical non-essential. Absolutely critical to its success, unexpected, yet given away from day one. Platforms also have to develop content and encourage third parties to do the same (Amazon reviews!).

TARGETED IDEATION

Very often the process of ideating new business opportunities is a mixture of realising that there is stuff on the bench that can be repurposed or gaps in provision that need to be filled and then a darkpool of unknowns. The bubble to the right of the diagram is the darkpool. There are all these things that need ideating around.

The ideation process has to include the kinds of long-tail tools that might attract an ecosystem or unlock customer demand (these will likely be giveaways and strategists find the idea of a give-away too counterintuitive); the likelihood is content will play a large role and tech-focused strategists stall when it comes to thinking about content. They do not understand its importance or how to create it. Customer-centricity strategies such as trust building will play a role but companies who have regarded customers as targets will struggle to make investments in real trust. As many assets as possible should be sharable. Design to share. Having tools that allow different parts of the ecosystem to embrace each other's activities (reviews for example) are easier to accept but they require an investment.

All this falls into the field of ideation. It is freeform, Wall-based, iterative with how you see your potential ecosystem and with your goals. So, more of those topics now.

THE ECOSYSTEM

Exploring missing assets, the things you don't have that might satisfy unmet needs, is the opportunity to explore how an ecosystem can evolve around you. We've already said above that many ecosystem partners do not touch the platform (Airbnb remote access support) or exploit the platform in surprising ways (search arbitrage). It is frustrating for executives, and difficult to accept, that some success factors will come by accident rather than design. However, providing the ecosystem with sufficient tools and ensuring the platform is as complete as it can be, allows the unknowns a chance to emerge. The point not to miss is that you have obvious ecosystem potential (co-suppliers) and not so obvious ones (arbitrage players, content providers etc).

CREATING GOALS FROM ASSETS

An analysis of assets can give you a few goals that comprise your first small steps to a big strategy.

- Identify new customer segments to discover hidden opportunity.

- Identify internal assets that are relevant to those new segments.

- Call out the missing assets and the dark pool.

- Identify an ecosystem that can deliver assets that are missing from your skill set.

- Ideate new tools and content to support an even broader eco-system, beyond a simple supplier base.

- Learn how to combine those assets in a way that is really appropriate for modern markets - using a Go To Market strategy that builds share-ability and advocacy into the product or service.

- Explore content and advocacy issues (social strategy, design to share, effects of a network).

These components might sound like they imply big projects but they do not. Using Flow principles, they can be designed into chunks that last a day or so. They can bring results fast. But step 1 is to state the goals.

Address those segments with unmet needs	Identify assets, missing, hidden, known	Understand ecosystem potential	Resolve internal deficits	Design for market (make features shareable)	Create content strategy

If you look back to Chapters 2 and 5 you will see that we recommend at this stage breaking work down under these goals. Your first iteration will give you a grasp of the important work areas, before you go on to create units of work.

What you now have is the beginnings of an ecosystem strategy for your agile business. It just has not been written as a strategy. It gets built from the discovery of assets, the iteration of goals, areas of work and units of work, and experience and feedback.

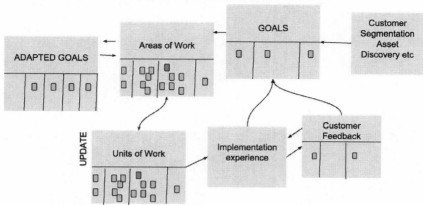

Asset discovery, goal adaptation, units of work and feedback

STRATEGY BUILDING FROM INCREMENTAL STEPS

Now think again about some of the comments we made earlier. There are critical non-essentials involved in any high performance arena. There are efficiencies to be gained by optimising across hundreds of small steps. We have talked also about optimising many marginal gains.

If you apply these thoughts to digital projects then you have the ultimate modern paradox. Highly scaled businesses built out of many small units of activity. What might those units be? Using Flow principles you would begin with the customer segmentation (Chapter 2) and asset discovery (just discussed). You can envision the walls of your office with a Customer Innovation Wall that depicts the segmentation. Alongside it you will have an inventory of assets (known, hidden, unknown-but-needed). Alongside that you could have a series of ideation A3s suggesting what tools and tricks you need if you are to engage customers and third parties in an ecosystem.

The creation of these Walls is no more than a couple of days each and it is conversational. There are no big planning periods. People do a small amount of research and then they get together. The discovery process and the identification of steps is an interactive conversation among people who want to create new value. It is an exercise in value-seeking behaviour.

As these conversations start to fill the Walls, it becomes apparent that there are some baseline actions - the next best actions that can go on the Wall (of course even these need a breakdown) because they obviously create value.

Address segments with unmet needs	Identify assets, missing, hidden, known	Embed in ecosystem	Resolve internal deficits	Design for market	Create content strategy
▢ ▢	▢ ▢ ▢	◼ ▢	▢	▢ ▢	◼ ▢ ▢

◼ Large work areas

▢ Medium work areas

▢ Small work areas

Assess by value $, $$, $$$
Identify beneficiary
Assign for breakdown

Some of the best next actions for the goals above would be written in a Twitter length statement on those cards you see in the table. They would have a value estimate attached to them. They might be:

1. Negotiate micro-transaction policy with finance (without it you won't be able to operate a platform).

2. Specify improvements for the SDK to make it more flexible for developers.

3. Dive deeper on 1-3 key customer segments to elicit more insights into opportunities for early market returns.

4.   Identify/engage with content experts

5.   Set up a Wall sequence beginning with high level objectives and begin the breakdown into goals and units of work as we described in Chapters 5 and 6.

These actions are a straightforward response to the need for a strategy. It is easy to list a dozen necessary actions to get the small steps underway. Each one of those actions will be broken down into smaller steps and you will be thinking about their value all the time.

For example: Resolving internal deficits involves negotiating a micropayments strategy with the CFO office, a key blocker. That can be broken down into three easy and short steps:

- Get examples of other companies that have moved to micropayments' management (success stories).

- Provide a brief ROI (number of micropayments, expansion in business opportunity).

- Show a plan and the CFOs key role in it (a two pager on the opportunity which raises the significance of the CFO as a decision maker).

All the other areas of work can be broken down similarly until you have a hundred small actions where people are talking about value. It is up to a team leader to manage these initiatives up the hierarchy. It is up to everybody to accept a short cycle-time and a disrupted cadence of work. Everything now will happen in two-day units maximum. Everything will be geared to finding value. One of those key value actions would be to understand how business ecosystems function. Very few companies have that insight. A good place to start a two day project would be describing the Amazon and Airbnb ecosystems. They both contain many clues to harnessing third party value.

Here is the process again, schematically:

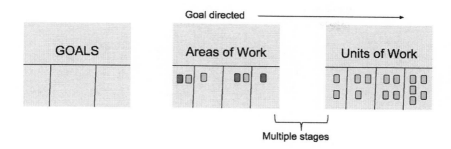

CONCLUSION

Most of the work we do today is work-in-progress. Never done. But a book has to end. We have pulled together some key components in this final chapter.

Work at all levels of the organisation is becoming less about excellence in execution and more about adaptability in the face of changing circumstances. When you can accept that order is best created by allowing people to codesign multiple strands of work, and that the big plan needs to be hundreds of small units of work, then you have the capacity to adapt, infinitely.

The challenge is that all of this rests on the shoulders of those people who have been empowered to do good work. Leaders can no longer administer the process or organise the hierarchical structure of execution. Empowerment means exactly what it says: Giving power to others. The surprising discovery waiting for many leaders is that the workforce, by and large, is ready for empowerment and able to codesign work very effectively.

The example we have just given, the development of Platform Strategy, the codesign and then execution of hundreds of work units, needs leaders who can see the whole picture. Instead of that old plan, which as we all know was always a fiction, they have to see what is emerging in all the value activity around them. Not even that is a lonely task. They have visualisations of all work and they have the power of conversation. All strategy will become good conversations over time. The future will be written on the Walls.

You need a passion for change to follow everything we have said. You need to believe in a movement built on small steps. Real empowerment in the modern workplace lies with you, not us. You are the co-author of change. We do hope Flow is of value. In the meantime, what are you going to change today?

ABOUT THE AUTHORS

Haydn Shaughnessy has advised and mentored startups and major institutions around the world. He has worked in the technology sector since the early 1990s but always with a view to how technology and people interact. He is a sociologist and economist by training and has written about the impact of technologies on business and work at Forbes, The Harvard Business Review, Gigaom, The Irish Times and Strategy and Leadership. He is also author of Shift: A Leader's Guide to the Platform Economy and with Fin; Flow: A Handbook for Change-Makers, Mavericks, Innovation Activists and Leaders.

Fin Goulding is International CIO at the insurance giant Aviva, where he is a member of the senior leadership team dragging a 300 year old organisation into the present. He has served in similar roles at the dotcom startup lastminute.com, Visa (US and Europe) and Paddy Power Betfair. He switches between the roles of CIO and CTO depending on the challenges he faces whether that is fixing the gaps in a startup when it scales or redeeming large organisations from the sins of the past. He has lead teams across Europe, the Americas and India, always bringing his greatest asset, trust in people and the power of their common sense when permitted to seek out value.

Thanks for being a reader of our book. If you have enjoyed *Flow* would you please leave a review on Amazon? However short, it will help other readers to discover the book. We are indebted to you.